THE CASE INTERVIEW WORKBOOK

*60 Case Questions for
Management Consulting
with Solutions*

The Case Interview Workbook

60 Cases for Management Consulting with Solutions

Copyright © Robert Mellon, 2018
All rights reserved.

Cover Design: Vanessa Mendozzi

ISBN: 978-1-72-370256-3

Published by STC Press

Contents

Introduction

This book fills a gap I discovered when preparing for management consulting interviews. Namely, that practice cases are both few and poor in quality. I managed to overcome this problem with help from friends, and ended up accepting an offer from McKinsey & Company. There, I interviewed many candidates and saw firsthand how many suffer from this lack of material.

This workbook is intended to fill this gap. It includes 60 case questions with complete solutions, compiled and edited by me as well as other ex-consultants. Many of the cases are from actual interviews at the top tier firms, i.e.

McKinsey, BCG and Bain, and unavailable elsewhere.

My path to a consulting offer

During my university studies, I decided that management consulting would be my first career choice. To improve my odds, I used almost every resource I could think of to prepare for the upcoming interviews. For the non-case parts, free online resources such as blog articles and forums were enough to know what I needed to do.

For the case part, I combined free online resources with the most popular prep books. Additionally, I used university casebooks to practice live cases with friends and schoolmates. However, while this proved to be enough to be somewhat prepared, one thing was always missing: a good collection of business cases to practice with.

Fortunately, I was lucky, as I had friends who were already working in consulting and were willing to help me. Over a period of a few weeks, I met with them regularly and we practiced dozens of cases together, many of which were actually used in past interviews at their firms.

This filled the final gap in my preparation and gave me confidence for the subsequent interviews. Consequently, I ended up receiving and accepting an offer from McKinsey, my first choice for an employer. Without the case practice sessions with my consulting friends, this would unlikely have been the case.

The gap in existing resources

From the inside, I could see that others were not as lucky. At the top-tier consulting firms, associates and more senior consultants interview new candidates. During my time at McKinsey, I interviewed many applicants over the following years. A clear pattern started to emerge: while many candidates did well on the non-case parts, a great majority struggled to solve the cases.

Clearly, there was a gap when it came to preparing for this part of the interview. In my view, the reason is that the most popular resources today do not incorporate adequate case practice. Let's go through them one by one:

- **Case in Point by Marc Cosentino**: This is a great book to gain a general overview of the consulting interview. Additionally, it is useful to prepare for brainteaser and estimation types of cases. However, the 12 frameworks outlined for solving business cases are too many to be realistically used. But most importantly, the cases in the book are not useful. The questions and solutions are mixed together as a conversation, which makes them nearly impossible to practice with, and the solutions are often illogical and unintuitive.

- **Case Interview Secrets by Victor Cheng**: This is a great resource, both for the non-case parts and also for frameworks to solve cases. The three frameworks outlined (profitability, business situation, M&A) can be used and adapted to many types of cases. However, there are no cases provided to actually practice with, so those need to be found elsewhere.

- **University casebooks:** The most popular way to fill the gaps left by these two books is to use casebooks from consulting clubs at universities. Although some of these cases can be good to practice with, the majority suffers from a lack of depth and quality. Moreover, the solutions are all too often incorrect. For a beginner, these books may do more harm than good. Thus, relying on casebooks leaves a candidate inadequately prepared.

- **Online forums and communities**: There are many online forums and communities with user submitted cases. The problem with these services is the same as with the casebooks: there is a lack of editorial oversight from actual consultants, so many of the questions and solutions are of poor quality.

The implication of this is that a candidate who uses all available resources is still likely to come poorly prepared for the business case part of his interview. It was because of this realization that I decided to write this book.

Filling the gap

This workbook finally fills the gap for case practice resources. I have collected in one place 60 cases of all types. Every case question and solution has been edited by me as well as friends and colleagues, all of us ex-consultants from McKinsey, BCG, and Bain. Many cases are from recent interviews at these firms, and cannot be found elsewhere. Together, this ensures relevance, depth, and quality of every question and solution.

Please note that this is a workbook, intended to be complementary to other resources. It does not teach you frameworks, how to use them, or how to structure solutions. These concepts are already well addressed by others, for example by the books Case in Point, Case Interview Secrets, and multiple free articles online. This workbook simply presents you with 60 cases which you can use to practice, either on your own or with friends and mentors.

However, before diving in immediately, I want to briefly outline the typical structure of consulting interviews, and the importance of case practice, to ensure you have the context to understand how this workbook can help you.

How consulting interviews work

Management consulting interviews are highly predictable. All three of the top tier firms, i.e. McKinsey, BCG, and Bain, ask similar types of questions, which only a slight emphasis difference between the three firms. This has the implication that candidates can prepare much better compared to conventional job interviews.

On the flip side, those who come inadequately prepared do not get far, as the lack of preparation quickly becomes apparent.

This high degree of predictability actually helps consulting firms distinguish candidates. Those who are truly committed to landing a job in consulting will demonstrate this commitment by devoting a significant amount of time to prepare. In contrast, those who do not share this high level of motivation will find it very difficult to devote as much time to the preparations. Because the process is so clearly defined, the consulting firms can identify those who are truly interested in the job by seeing which candidates put in the necessary work.

The interview structure

Consulting interviews can be divided into four distinct parts: (1) motivation, (2) personal experience, (3) case questions, (4) candidate questions. Below follows a brief description and example questions for each of these parts. Every question below has been asked in a real interview at McKinsey, BCG, or Bain. If you are not familiar with consulting interviews, this will help you get a feel for what they are like.

Part 1: Motivation

The first part of the interview is designed to test your motivation. This is done by seeing how you answer questions about your reasons for applying, and how you relate your background to the role. This part usually consists of approximately three questions, each testing a slightly different thing.

The first motivational question is usually common and easy to prepare for. This is on purpose, as it helps good candidates start the interview with some momentum, so they can demonstrate their abilities later on. Examples:

- Why do you want to work in consulting?
- Why do you want to work for us?
- Tell us a little bit about yourself.

The second question goes deeper than the first one, seeing how well prepared you are in terms of less obvious questions. Examples:

- Can you walk us through your CV?
- What do you consider your strengths?
- What do you consider your weaknesses?
- What do you think consultants do?

Finally, there is often a third question in the motivational part. Sometimes these questions are negative or unusually direct, to see if you can reframe the answer positively under stress. Examples:

- Why should we hire you?
- Which other firms are you interviewing with and why?
- What will you do if we do not hire you?

Part 2: Personal experience

Personal stories are the second part of the interview. You should be prepared to talk about your past in a detailed way, outlining how you met a specific challenge, the actions you took, and the results. The three most common themes asked about are leadership, impact on others, and personal achievement. Examples:

- Tell us about a significant personal achievement.
- Tell us about a time you changed someone's mind.
- Tell us about a time you led others.
- Tell us about a time you had team problems, and how you dealt with it.

- Tell us about a time you had to work with someone who you didn't get along with.

Part 3: Case questions

Case questions are the third part of the interview. This part requires by far the most time to prepare for, as you can encounter many different types of questions. Generally, a so-called estimation question is included. Here, you are expected to make assumptions and demonstrate your mental math skills to reach a reasonable estimate. Examples:

- How many smartphones were sold globally last year?
- What is the market size for light bulbs in the UK?
- How many piano tuners are in Chicago?
- How many beer bottles are currently in circulation in the US?
- How many cups of coffee are sold in Germany each year?

Following an estimate question is a more open-ended case question. You are expected to outline the path you will take to solve the question (the framework), ask for the information you feel you need to solve the case, and proceed to give a summary and a recommendation in the end. Examples:

- Your client manufactures a commodity (gasoline for example). They are the market leader and are the lowest cost producer. The CEO wants to increase profits in the next 3 months. What would be your recommendation about how to achieve this?
- A small R&D lab in the Swiss Alps has developed a super-durable filament for light bulbs; with this filament, the light bulb will never burn out. The lab is ready to license this product to a light bulb manufacturer. What will be the effect on the light bulb industry?
- Your client is a US firm which owns a meat packing plant in Spain. Over the last few periods profits at this plant have steadily declined, despite growing sales. What is the reason?
- One of the partners at your firm has just walked down the hall and asked us to look into a question he wants to address in a pitch for new business. He received a call from the CEO of a national airline based on the west

coast. The CEO wants to increase his company's profits and would like us to see what impact having an additional passenger on every flight would have and what it would take to achieve this goal.

- Your client is the largest North American producer of a certain kind of bubble-pack packaging material. Currently, the company has 80% of the market, and has asked your firm to assess the strategic outlook for this company. How would you begin to assess the future for this client, and what type of recommendations could you make?

Part 4: Candidate questions

In the fourth, and final, part of the interview, you are expected to ask questions of your own. You should ask about things which demonstrate that you have done your homework and are interested in participating in the work that goes on at the firm. Example questions which indicate this are:

- Do you have any questions for us?
- Is there anything you would like to know before we conclude?

How to prepare

Now you have a clear idea about the structure of your upcoming interview. Of these four different parts, the third part – the case interview – requires by far the most preparation. There are over a dozen different types of case questions which can be encountered, and arguably even more, as each case is usually unique in some way. Thus, the case interview part will truly separate those who have done their homework from those who haven't.

The question then becomes on how to prepare effectively. Reading books, articles, and blog posts will get you far with the other parts, but for the case questions, it is ineffective on its own. The most rewarding way to prepare for the case interview is to combine reading with practice by solving real cases.

Case practice gradually builds the skills required: identifying the type of case encountered, which framework to use, which questions to ask, and how to structure and deliver the best response.

Following are 60 case questions and solutions you can use to do precisely that. Don't just read through all the questions and solutions. Instead, practice with someone who can give the case to you before you look at the solution. Alternatively, you can read the question, think about your answer, and write it down before looking at the solution.

Additionally, I recommend that you distribute the work of solving the cases over a few days or weeks, and regularly review the solutions afterwards. This will help you with retaining and internalizing what you have learned.

Finally, a disclaimer. This is a *workbook*, designed to accompany other learning resources. You will not be able to solve the cases without learning first elsewhere how to approach and solve business cases. For that, I recommend the books mentioned earlier in this introduction.

Practice Cases

On the following pages are 60 case questions and solutions. They are designed to be of somewhat similar length, so very long problems are split up to two cases, and very short problems may be grouped together into one case.

To get the most out of the cases, make sure to choose a framework and formulate any clarifying questions before looking at the "information to be given if asked" part. Then, see if you can solve the case before looking at the solution. Both will be easier if you have a practice partner who can give the case to you.

Case #1: Gasoline

Question

This question was asked by McKinsey in a 2nd round interview.

Your client manufactures a commodity (gasoline for example). They are the market leader and are the lowest cost producer. The CEO wants to increase profits in the next 3 months. What would be your recommendation about how to achieve this?

Solution

Key observation

The key to solving this case is using the fact that demand for commodities is highly inelastic. Commodities are essential for consumers, which means that changes in prices have little effect on demand. As an example, if the price of gasoline increases by 25 percent in one day, drivers wouldn't be very happy about it, but they would still fill up their tanks, because they need gas to get to work, run errands, etc.

In the longer term, demand for commodities becomes more elastic, as people adapt to the price by changing their behavior. Continuing with our gasoline example, higher prices would lead to people buying cars with better fuel economy, and electric car technologies becoming more viable, leading to reduced demand.

Since this case is focused on the next three months, you can fully ignore these long-term effects and assume that demand for the commodity is highly inelastic. Using this assumption, you proceed to solve the case:

Framework and solution

We want to increase profits, so you use the following framework to determine the best way to do this:

Profits = Revenues – Cost

We have already established that the client is the lowest cost producer, hence the costs cannot be lowered any further. Your solution will thus focus on increasing revenues. You can decompose revenues like so:

Revenues = Price x Quantity

You should assume that the client is running at maximum capacity utilization, so quantity cannot be increased in the short term. This leads to the conclusion that the only solution is to increase price.

To determine the price, use the framework of supply and demand. The two ways to increase price are to increase demand or to decrease supply. Due to the commodity nature of the product, it is unlikely that the demand can be increased significantly in the short run. Hence, focus on supply.

Now you need to draw the supply and demand
curves to show the effects visually:

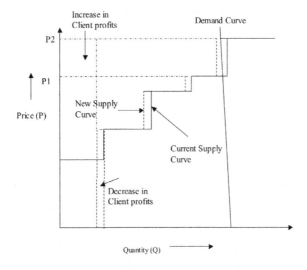

Using this diagram, you should make the
recommendation to the client to decrease its
capacity utilization. This will cause the supply
curve to shift towards the left, increasing the
market clearing price from P1 to P2.

You should point out the two boxes showing the
increase (due to higher price) and decrease (due
to lower quantity) in client profits. The increase
outweighs the decrease here.

How to prepare

This is an industry analysis case, where you are expected to understand basic dynamics of microeconomics, i.e. competition and consumer behavior. Ensure that you have a good understanding of the concepts included in this solution: price elasticity, economic commodities, supply and demand curves, and capacity utilization.

Various other variants of a case like this can come up in an interview, for example when products are differentiated instead of commodities, or if the industry is a monopoly or an oligopoly. These are all concepts from microeconomics, and we will cover with other cases in the coming days and weeks.

Case #2: Direct mail

Question

You are consulting for a direct mail retailer that sells women's clothing. Your client's catalog printing and postage costs have just increased to thirty-two cents per catalog. How can your client decide if the new price is acceptable?

Please note

When you are asked a question with missing information, you are expected to ask clarifying questions before attempting to solve the case. For this case, the information in the bullet points below will be given to you by the interviewer if you ask.

Formulate the questions you want to ask before looking at the information below. This way, you can test your ability to approach a case where much of the information is missing.

Information to be given if asked

• The average response rate for catalogs mailed is 2%

- In addition, 25% of customers who order product can be expected to reorder within six months
- In other words, each 100 catalogs mailed results in 2.5 orders place.
- The average order size is $80
- The fully allocated profit margin (excluding mailing costs) on catalog orders is 15%.

Solution

In order to answer the question, you need to estimate the revenues per catalog to know whether they exceed the cost. The key is to ask for the right information, and not for more than you need.

Using all the information provided by the interviewer, you can then go through the following steps to estimate the revenues:

- For each 100 catalogs mailed, printing and postage costs are $32. (100 x 32 cents).
- Each 100 catalogs will result in 2 orders, plus 2 x 25%, or .5 additional reorders, for a total of 2.5 orders placed per 100 catalogs mailed.
- 5 orders will result in 2.5 x 80, or $200 in sales. At a profit margin of fifteen percent, these sales will return a total profit of $30.
- The $30 profit is not sufficient to cover the printing and mailing costs of $32. Therefore, the client should reject the printing arrangement at 32 cents per copy.

You should go through these steps out loud, calculating all the numbers in your head and walking the interviewer through the solution, until you reach the conclusion.

How to prepare

This is an estimation case. Here, the main skills tested are: 1) asking for the right information, 2) calculating the numbers easily while communicating clearly.

If you had a hard time calculating numbers in your head, practice your mental math. This skill is tested to some degree in most cases, and there are plenty of free tools online to achieve this.

Case #3: R&D lab

Question

This is an industry analysis case.

A small R&D lab in the Swiss Alps has developed a super-durable filament for light bulbs; with this filament, the light bulb will never burn out. The lab is ready to license this product to a light bulb manufacturer. What will be the effect on the light bulb industry?

Information to be given if asked

- The light bulb industry is dominated by two multinational producers. The two companies sell their products side by side for essentially the same price in similar outlets internationally.
- There are a several small local players in various regions of the world who produce local brands and some private store brand light bulbs.
- There have been no technological innovations in light bulbs for many years.

Solution

You should outline two possible outcomes.

One outcome is that one of the two major players purchases the technology. If the technology is patented and exclusively licensed, this player may enjoy an advantage for a limited time. If the producer makes enough bulbs at a low enough cost, all customers will eventually switch over to the permanent light bulb, thereby drying up the industry, putting the competitor out of business and greatly reducing their own business.

Another solution is that all of the players obtain some version of this technology. If that were to happen, the price for this product would decline to the normal industry profit level, and customers would shift to the permanent light bulb. Over time, all bulbs would be permanent and the industry volume would greatly decrease, making the industry more competitive and wiping out industry profits.

How to prepare

This is a strategy case, where the solution depends on a good insight into competitive dynamics and fundamental microeconomics. You need to be comfortable with qualitative cases of this type, where no numbers are provided and you are still expected to provide valuable insights. One of the best ways is to practice with different variants of these types of cases, which are provided in this book.

Case #4: Hertz

Question

You are consulting for Hertz, a global car rental company present on the European and North American markets. In Europe, it is present in most EU countries but has not yet entered the Baltic countries.

Hertz has asked us to determine whether or not they should enter the Baltic market (Estonia, Latvia and Lithuania being here considered as one market).

1) In the introductory meeting with Hertz's European director, he asks you how you plan to approach the problem. Give a brief description of the key areas you want to focus on to analyze the problem.

2) Based on your proposed approach, how would you go about conducting the analysis and gathering the information required?

3) After gathering the data, you have the information outlined below to help with the market entry analysis. Hertz is looking at a net profit target of at least $200k after the initial 3

years. How much market share does Hertz need
to capture in the Baltic to reach their target?

- Total Size of Car Rental Market in Baltic:
  $10m
- Annual Market Growth: 10%
- Industry Net Profit Margin: 5%

Solution

1) Expected here is an answer along the 3 C's where the candidate focuses on:

- Market
- Size of the market
- Growth rate
- Segmentation
- Competition
- How many competitors?
- Respective market shares
- Differentiation factors
- Alternative competitors/substitutes
- Consumers
- Type of consumers: business, tourist, local
- Segmentation
- Trend in consumer demand
- Capabilities/Core strengths
- Brand
- Corporate agreements/Customer Loyalty programme

Any framework suggested is expected to cover the basics: industry & market, competition, and customer needs - with regards to gaps and core strengths/capabilities of the client firm.

2) This question tests your initiative and if you can think about whether data is easily available or not. Good answers would include:

- Buy market and competitive research
- Observation of competitors operations (sampling and then extrapolation)
- Leverage knowledge of other European markets to determine consumer segmentation and trends in consumer demand

3) Using the provided information, you should do the following calculation in your head while communicating it out loud:

- Market size after 3 years: approx. $13m
- Total industry profit will be $650k ($13m x 5%)
- To reach a target of $200k in net profit, Hertz would need about 1/3 market share in 3 years

How to prepare

Ensure that you have a good grip on common frameworks used for market analysis. Using them when you encounter open questions like this ensures that you cover the most important factors in a structured manner. If you do this well, the follow-up questions also become easier.

Case #5: Magazine

Question

Your client is the CEO of a publishing company that produces a line of educational magazines as well as a line of women's magazines. Both businesses are profitable but are not growing quickly. He wants to start a third monthly magazine in the US targeted at 30-50-year-old men (e.g. GQ Magazine). His stated goal is to generate circulation revenues of $10 million in the first year. He has hired you to figure out whether this is possible.

Solution

Context

This is an estimation case. The key here is to clearly define your approach and assumptions, the specific answer is less important than making reasonable assumptions. Outline the high-level steps you will take before diving into the mental math, and use them to guide the interviewer through your solution.

Example solution

To estimate the potential revenues, estimate first the total market, then potential market share, and finally, revenues resulting from that market share:

1) Total Market: The total US population is approximately 320 million. Assume an average life span of 80 years and an equal age distribution up until the age of 60, with half the density above that age. So, 90% of the people fall between the ages of 0-60, and 30% between 30-50. Half of those are male, so 15% of the population, or approximately 50 million, falls into the target group.

Of the 50 million 30-50-year-old men in the country, assume that at least 1/2 would read a magazine or 25 million. Given the wide range of magazines on the market assume that only 10% of magazine readers would want to read a men's journal or 2.5 million target customers.

2) Market Share: As a new magazine, assume that you can generate a 5% share of the men's magazine market in year one or 120,000 customers.

3) Revenues: Based on what other magazines sell for ($2.50-$5.00) assume a cover price. Let's say $3/magazine at the newsstand and $2/magazine for a subscription. Now make some assumptions on how many customers will buy on the newsstand versus subscription, let's say 50% subscribe (60,000) and 50% buy at the news stand (60,000). This comes out to $180,000 + $120,000 or $300,000. Finally, this is a monthly magazine. For simplicity assume that all target customers buy a magazine every month. This would generate total revenues of $300,000 X 12 or $3.6 million.

Conclusion: In this case, given the CEO's stated goal of $10 million in circulation revenues, it would not make sense to launch the magazine.

Case #6: Meat packing

Question

Your client is a US firm which owns a meat packing plant in Spain. Over the last few periods profits at this plant have steadily declined, despite growing sales. You have been hired to figure out why.

Information to be given if asked:

- The suppliers are independent farmers with little power against your client
- The market is fairly regional; hence transportation costs and competition have not changed dramatically
- No substitute product has been introduced
- Production costs have remained stable

Solution

Begin by selecting an appropriate framework. Porter's Five Forces is a good framework to use here, as it allows you to see whether external factors are affecting industry profitability. Furthermore, you can also use a profitability framework to identify internal factors.

Using these frameworks, you first ask whether there is any information available on each of the Five Forces. You will learn that suppliers still have little power, no substitute product has been introduced, and the industry rivalry/competition is unchanged. Hence, there is no apparent external factor reducing your profitability.

Using the profitability framework (Profit = Quantity * Price - Costs), you ask whether costs have changed, and get the reply that they remain unchanged. As sales have been growing, you conclude that the reason for declining profitability must be the price of your product.

Using the Five Forces framework again, this leads you to discovering the buyer link. Your margins are being squeezed due to increasing concentration and buying power of your customers.

Case #7: Glass bottles

Question

A glass manufacturer in China which sells bottles to customers has come up with the following graph:

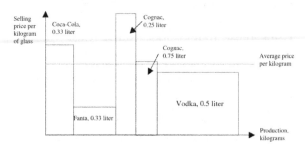

According to the graph, price per kilogram of 0.25-liter cognac bottle is much higher than the price per kilogram of 0.75-liter cognac bottle. Based on this information, the manufacturer wants to switch one of its production lines from 0.75-liter bottles to 0.25-liter.

Is this a good idea?

<u>Information to be given if asked:</u>

- There are no production constraints

- There are no problems with selling: everything they produce they can sell
- The weight of a bottle is proportionate to its volume
- Production costs can be assumed to be completely fixed
- Unit production capacity is slightly lower for larger bottles

Solution

This case tests your understanding of economics, operations, as well as your common sense.

A tempting solution would be to immediately say yes, because the bar for the 0.25-liter bottles is much taller, but you should never jump to a conclusion before evaluating all available facts.

So, the best way is to begin by finding out whether there is any additional information available.

The main clue you have been given is in the label for the y-axis: the selling price is denoted in kilograms of glass, but not in units sold, which seems unusual. You can start by stating that before proceeding, you want to understand this better. For example, do all the bottles weigh the same, or do they have different weights?

The interviewer replies that the weight of a bottle is proportional to its volume.

From this information, you should immediately see that the revenue per bottle is actually higher for the 0.75-liter bottle. Conveying this insight, you state that the estimated revenues per bottle are approximately 50% higher for the 0.75-liter bottle compared to the 0.25-liter bottle.

Having established the revenues, you now need to figure out the costs by understanding the production process. Begin by asking whether you know anything about the production costs. The interviewer replies that production costs can be assumed to be completely fixed. Hence, the mix of bottles produced does not affect the costs of running the plant.

Here you should also refrain from jumping immediately to a conclusion. Despite higher revenues and the same costs for the larger bottles, production capacity always plays a role in manufacturing. So you ask the interviewer how the manufacturing process works. Are some bottles more time consuming to manufacture, leading to lower production capacity?

The interviewer replies that production capacity is slightly lower for larger bottles, i.e. they take a little bit more time to produce.

Still refraining from an early recommendation, you examine whether any other constraints are limiting the manufacturer from switching between production lines. Are there any constraints with demand, pricing, or production limiting their ability to switch between lines?

The interviewer replies that there are no such constraints: they can produce anything they want and everything they can produce they can sell without affecting the price.

Now you know everything you need to make a recommendation: as the revenue per bottle is significantly higher for the larger bottles, the costs the same, and capacity only slightly lower, the profitability from the larger bottles is actually higher than from the smaller ones.

Using some numbers to verify your conclusion, you run the following numbers through a profitability framework:

(Price * Units) - Costs = Profit

Smaller bottles: (10 * 10) - 50 = 50

Larger bottles: (15 * 8) - 50 = 70

This estimation supports your conclusion: switching production to the smaller bottles is a bad idea.

Case #8: Airline passenger

Question

One of the partners at your firm has just walked down the hall and asked us to look into a question he wants to address in a pitch for new business. He received a call from the CEO of a national airline based on the west coast. The CEO wants to increase his company's profits and would like us to see what impact having an additional passenger on every flight would have and what it would take to achieve this goal.

Data to be given by interviewer if asked:

- The airline operates for 16 hours per day
- There are two planes on each route
- The following information is available for the routes:

City pair	Average one-way fare	Total time *(including load / unload)*	% of flights
LAX-SFO	$100	2 hours	40%
LAX-SEA	$250	3 hours	25%
LAX-ORD	$500	4 hours	20%
LAX-JFK	$600	6 hours	15%

Solution

Begin by stating that you will answer the two questions one by one, starting with the impact of an additional passenger on every flight.

1. Impact of an additional passenger

Start with the profitability framework (Profit = Revenues - Cost), discussing what the effects will be in those terms. You should realize (and confirm with the interviewer) that the addition of one passenger has negligible impact on the cost of the flight. Therefore, each additional passenger's revenue goes directly to the bottom line.

Before starting to calculate the additional revenues, you should also make sure that there is capacity to add additional passengers on all flights, by confirming this with the interviewer.

You should also realize that information on the number of flights on each route is missing, so you ask about it. The interviewer tells you that two planes operate on each route, and that all planes operate for 16 hours per day.

Now you can move on to estimating the numbers. The additional daily revenue from each passenger on every flight is the ticket price times the number of flights per day:

- LAX-SFO: 2 planes * 16 hours of operation / 2 hours per route = 16 flights per day
- LAX-SEA: 2 * 16 / 3 = 10.7 ≈ 11 flights
- LAX-ORD: 2 * 16 / 4 = 8 flights
- LAX-JFK: 2 * 16 / 6 ≈ 6 flights

So daily revenues are:

- LAX-SFO: 16 * 100 = 1600
- LAX-SEA: 11 * 250 = 2750
- LAX-ORD: 8 * 500 = 4000
- LAX-JFK: 6 * 600 = 3600
- Total: 12,000 USD per day

Assuming the airline operates 360 days per year, this amounts to 12,000 * 360 = 4.32 million USD per passenger per year.

In relative terms, if each plane has a capacity for 200 passengers, and 80% of the seats are occupied on average, an additional passenger will increase revenues by 1 / 160 = 0.6%.

2. What it would take to achieve this goal

You should discuss main levers to increase the number of passengers, e.g. advertising, promotions, partnerships, fare-sales, etc. You can also mention price or service as two important but opposing levers available for increasing passengers. Finally, you could segment into two passenger types (business & leisure) and discuss differences in price sensitivity.

Moving beyond the question to the actual goal, you could also think about what the ultimate goal is (i.e. increased profit), and talk about how it might be easier to cut costs than increase revenue. Ideas here could include reducing turn time, partnerships with other airlines, sales of ancillary products/services (e.g. food), or other operational improvements.

Case #9: Utility collections

Question

A collections department of a utility company has hired you to help. They have two means of receiving payments from customers. The first way is online, which accounts for 90% of their billings. The second way is a collections office located downtown. Presently it costs them $0.10 per bill to collect online but $1.20 per bill through the office they operate downtown. They have hired you to help them reduce the cost per bill of the agency. What would you do?

Solution

This is a case where you need to have a structured discussion with your interviewer. First, always clarify whether your client is talking about 90% of sales volume or sales revenue. In this case, it does not matter.

Inquire about why it is so critical to keep this costly facility open for such a small percentage of their sales. It turns out your client is very loyal to its customers who prefer to use this walk-up facility.

Explore what other uses your client can use the facility for to generate revenue to spread out these costs. It turns out there are two big rooms in the back that they already rent out to local clubs so that has no potential impact on helping cover costs.

Is there a cheaper area for this building to be located? It turns out that the answer is no. Your client likes the present location given its proximity to its customers.

How does your client's competition operate its collection facilities? Do they have similar problems? Is it possible to outsource at a cheaper cost? No, it turns out your client is the only one to have this sort of operation.

Explore the cost associated with this building. It turns out the facility has long since been paid for and has very little overhead cost. It staffs 5 people all the time. (Hint, is there always enough demand to warrant 5 personnel?) It turns out they are not always that busy and can have fewer shifts throughout the month. This brings the cost per bill down to $1.00.

Examine all the functions this office serves. It turns out your client uses this facility to also open customer accounts and as a customer service center. This is the main issue of the case; your client should be splitting the cost per bill in three because this complex serves three different functions.

This gets the cost per bill down to $0.30 per bill, which is as low as you can get.

Case #10: Piano tuners

Question

How many piano tuners are there in Chicago?

Solution

This is arguably the most famous estimation question, and it frequently asked in some form by firms today. As with other problems of this type, the important thing is to make reasonable assumptions and be confident in your mental math. Let's go through an example solution:

You start by making the following assumptions:

- There are approximately 10 million people living in Chicago
- On average, there are two persons in each household
- Roughly one household in twenty has a piano that is tuned regularly
- Pianos that are tuned regularly are tuned about once per year
- It takes a piano tuner two hours to tune a piano, including travel time
- A piano tuner works for 8 hours per day, 5 days per week, 50 weeks per year

From these assumptions, you can calculate your estimate:

- Number of pianos tuned per year: 10m / (2 *
  20) = 250k
- Annual tunings per piano tuner: (8h / 2h) * 5 *
  50 = 1000
- Thus, there are 250 piano tuners in Chicago.

Case #11: Conglomerate

Question

This question was asked by McKinsey in a 2nd round interview.

Your client is a large multinational conglomerate with multiple plants globally. They were formed through mergers and acquisitions of many small firms over the last decade and there are still integration issues. The CEO would like to increase the ROIC of the firm from 10% to 20% in 3 years. Is it possible and how would you achieve this?

Information to be given if asked:

ROIC Definition

- ROIC is Return on Invested Capital. This can be achieved by growing the profits of the firm and/or by decreasing the invested capital.
- There are firms in the industry that have 20-30% ROIC. Hence the client's target looks achievable.

Competitive Landscape

- This is a highly fragmented industry with 20,000 competitors.

Customers

- Client has 30% customers in Europe, 10% in Asia, 50% in North America and 10% in ROW.
- The client has 2 types of products – Standard (almost a commodity) and Engineered (designed specifically for the client).
- The standard products are getting commoditized, hence have significant price pressure.
- The engineered products have good margins in the 1st year and then the margins decrease in subsequent 3-4 years.
- The client has 30,000 SKUs in their product portfolio.
- The industries that the client serves are as follows:

Industry	% of revenues	Standard product	Engineered product
Automotive	55%	65%	35%
Electronics	25%	45%	55%
Construction	10%	75%	25%
Others	10%	70%	30%

Solution

This is an operations/profitability question. The first thing to keep in mind is to clarify anything that you are not sure about. If you don't remember or know what ROIC stands for, there is nothing wrong with asking what it means. Proceeding from there, what you want to increase is the following:

Profits / Invested capital

You could use many different strategy frameworks to explore this problem. In this example, we will use the 3 Cs, assessing the Company, Competitors, and Customers:

Starting with the company, you are expected to pick up on the hint in the question, which states that there are integration issues from past acquisitions. Asking about what these issues are, the interviewer replies that while the specifics are beyond the scope of this case, there are indeed opportunities to integrate these companies better, decreasing cost through economies of scale and improving coordination.

You continue inquiring about the company, asking for information on other important factors, i.e. their competitive advantage, profitability (information on revenues and costs), plant capacity, distribution, management, etc. The interviewer tells you that none of this information is available. So, you and the Company part by mentioning that a potential lever for improving ROIC would be to reassess the number and locations of the client's plants, which would be a part of their integration issues.

Moving on to the Competitors part, you inquire about the industry. Is it consolidated or fragmented? The interviewer tells you that the industry is highly fragmented, with 20,000 competitors. Are any of these competitors achieving the target that the CEO would like to reach? Yes, there are firms with 20-30% ROIC. So, you conclude that the target seems achievable.

Finally, you move to the Customers. What types of customers does the client have, and do we have any segmentations available, i.e. by product, industry or geography? The interviewer supplies all three segmentations: with the table above, and by telling you that 30% of customers are in Europe, 10% in Asia, 50% in North America and 10% in rest of the world.

You ask about the economics of the two different types of products. The interviewer tells you that the Standard product is almost a commodity, while the Engineered product is designed specifically for the client, with high margins in the first year of sales, but lower after 3-4 years. Furthermore, the interviewer tells you that in total, there are 30,000 SKUs offered by your client.

Now you can make some concrete recommendations. Examining the table, you state that revenues from Electronics are quite low despite the industry having the highest % of Engineered products. The client should focus more on that industry.

Furthermore, you state that 30,000 SKUs seems very high, and the client should explore ways to reduce this number, which could reduce capital invested in development, manufacturing equipment, and inventories. One way would be to evaluate the profitability of each product and its importance for the total product portfolio. Production of commoditized products could be divested or outsourced to reduce the capital invested.

The interviewer tells you that you have identified enough opportunities for now and asks you to summarize your recommendations. In response, you state that you have identified four potential levers to improve ROIC:

- Improve integration of acquired companies to realize economies of scale and increase coordination
- Evaluate the capacity utilization and supply chain for the plants, comparing them for example to the geographical distribution of customers, reducing investment if possible
- Divest or outsource production of commoditized products to reduce investment and improve profitability of the product portfolio
- Focus on selling more of Engineered products, i.e. by growing in the Electronics industry

Case #12: Bubble gum

Question

Your client is the largest North American producer of a certain kind of bubble-pack packaging material. Currently, the company has 80% of the market, and has asked your firm to assess the strategic outlook for this company. How would you begin to assess the future for this client, and what type of recommendations could you make?

<u>Information to be given if asked</u>

Costs

- The product costs can be broken down as follows:
- 20% for polyethylene, a plastic chemical
- 35% conversion costs, including allocated fixed costs, labor and energy costs 10% distribution and storage
- 15% marketing and overhead.
- Profit margins are 20%. Polyethylene is a commodity chemical.

Technology

The factory is thirty years old, and the technology used is the same as when the factory opened.

Market/Competitors

The client had 100% of the market until two years ago. Since that time, a localized upstart company has appeared in the Philadelphia / New Jersey market and has captured nearly all of that market. This factory has purchased technology from a German company. Your client does not have much information about this competitor, but it appears that their factory is extremely efficient. They have also been undercutting your client on price.

Solution

The most challenging part about this case is unearthing the available information. If you achieve this, the solution itself is straightforward.

Using the 3 Cs framework, you work your way through the most relevant questions, which should unearth the information provided above in a similar manner as outlined in yesterday's solution. Once you are done with this, you reach the following conclusion:

The competitor has used their new technology to produce a lower price product. As evidenced in the Philadelphia / New Jersey market, nearly all customers prefer this product to your client's. Therefore, the future is bleak for your client, and they should respond immediately to the competitive threat, perhaps by updating their own technology.

Case #13: PC labs

Question

A provider of PC labs for use in schools in the US is looking to enter the UK market. The company has developed a somewhat innovative business model, whereby secondary schools are provided with up to 15 PCs. The PCs come fitted with e-learning software, which is structured and indexed by subject matter and level of education – e.g., GCSEs, Advanced Level, etc. The main source of revenue relates to advertising revenues generated through the display of banner ads on the screen. These ads are displayed when the PCs are in use during the school day. Advertisers in the US include McDonald's and the US Army. The company has developed long-term leasing arrangements with the main hardware suppliers (e.g., Dell, HP, etc.) and is therefore able to offer the kitted-out PC lab at no or a very minimal cost to schools.

Our first requirement was to determine the extent of the revenue opportunity for the company's proposition in the UK. What are the key inputs and assumptions that we would need to consider in order to determine potential revenues? And using these assumptions, what revenues would the company generate in Year 1?

Solution

There are a number of key inputs that you should consider. A good solution will also show evidence of sound commercial judgement when thinking through any key assumptions. Also, split your solution clearly into assumptions first, and revenue calculations afterwards, as the interviewer asked you to structure your response this way:

1. The key inputs and assumptions needed to estimate revenue are as follows:

- The number of secondary schools in the UK. Using rough assumptions, we assume that secondary school takes five years, the UK population is 80 million and age distribution is uniform between 0 and 80 years. Thus, there are 5 million students in secondary school. Assuming an average capacity of 1000 students, there are 5,000 secondary schools in the UK.
- The proportion of secondary schools signed up in Year 1. In order to keep the maths simple, we will assume that 10% are signed up in Year 1. We also assume that these 500

schools are customers from the start of the year.

- The number of PCs per school. Let's assume that each school will be fitted with one PC lab, with each lab having 15 PCs.
- The average daily use of each PC. Let's assume 5 hours per day – equivalent to a typical school day.
- The number of ads displayed in a day. Here, let's assume that each ad lasts on average, 30 seconds.
- The price of each ad. Let's assume a rate of £10 CPM (cost per mille) or £10 per 1,000 ads displayed.
- The number of weeks each year when the school (and therefore the PC lab) is open. Here, let's assume 40 weeks per annum (or 200 days, assuming a 5-day school week).
- The utilisation rate, i.e. the proportion of ad slots the provider manages to sell. Here, we shall assume a 50% utilisation.

2. Using these assumptions, we can now estimate the revenue in Year 1:

- With an average daily PC usage of 5 hours, and 15 PCs per school, each school uses 75 PC-hours per day
- Each ad is displayed for 30 seconds, so 120 ads can be displayed per hour, or 120 * 75 = 9,000 ads per school per day
- With a 50% utilization, 4,500 ads are actually displayed per day
- With 200 school days per year, total ads displayed per year are 4,500 * 200 = 900,000
- So yearly ad revenue per school is £0.01 * 900,000 = £9,000
- With 500 schools signed up, total ad revenue in Year 1 is £9,000 * 500 = £4.5 million

Case #14: PC labs, continued

Question

This case is a continuation of the previous case.

In order to validate our Year 1 revenue estimate, the next stage of this project is to try and determine the size of the advertising market targeting teenagers in the UK. Teenagers were the primary target demographic group (given the focus on secondary schools). This information would be used to determine what proportion of the teenage advertising market would be accounted for by our revenue projection for the company. Given this background, what methodologies could be used to size the teenage advertising market?

Solution

This question tests your ability to choose a good approach for market sizing, in addition to your estimation skills. Before diving into a particular method, you should outline all potential approaches you can think of, before choosing one or two to actually go with.

Here are examples of two different methods to make this estimation:

<u>Method 1: Advertising as a % of spending</u>

This approach is based around the total amount spent by teenagers in the UK. Key steps are as follows:

1. Determine the number of teenagers in the UK. Teenagers represent ~10% of UK population or ~8 million teenagers.

2. Determine average annual spending by teenager. Consider pocket money, earnings, cash gifts, etc. Here we assume that this amounts to just over £400 per month, or £5,000 per year.

3. If total teenage spending is 8 million * £5,000 = £40 billion, what is the advertising ratio – i.e., the amount spent on advertising by advertisers as a

proportion of total spending? Definitely less than 10%. Let's say 5%.

4. Total teenage market is about £2 billion

The analysis of the teenage advertising market provides a useful sense check of the Year 1 revenue estimate, which at £4.5 million, represents a relatively small proportion of the overall teenage ad market.

Method 2: Different Media

This approach is based on estimating the quantity and price of current advertising in different media to determine the size of the market.

1. Determine the different types of media used for advertising to teenagers. For example:

- TV
- Magazines
- Radio
- Newspapers
- Internet
- Billboards
- Other (buses, trains, London Underground, etc)

2. Focusing on the one medium, review a sample of publications or ads targeted at teenagers. For example, we can take a sample of teenage magazines.

3. Calculate the total revenue generated by ads in these magazines (based on number of ads, and prices obtained from the magazines or ad agencies).

4. Factor this total revenue figure up based on sample size.

5. Determine the proportion of total teenager advertising found in magazines. For example, how much time do teenagers spend reading magazines, compared to watching TV, surfing the web, etc.

6. Running the numbers would give a numerical estimate. If asked to do so, you could make an assumption about each factor. The formula would be this: (Quantity of Teen Magazine Ads * Price of Teen Magazine Ads) / (Sample Proportion of Total Magazines * Magazine Share of Teen Advertising)

Case #15: Drug launch

Question

Your client, XYZ Pharma is a large pharmaceutical manufacturer in the United States. It has recently launched Axeles, a cardiovascular drug that has proven to be the best of its class amongst its peers in FDA testing. Axeles launched a year ago and, despite its effectiveness, its sales have been considerably short of target and it has a much lower market share than the competitors. In fact, the company as a whole has been losing market share for other products as well but the focus is squarely on Axeles, as the analysts see it as a make-or-break product for the company's dwindling stock. The client has approached you to investigate the issue. The CEO feels if they can crack why Axeles is not doing well, they may be able to understand the issues facing the company as a whole.

Information given by interviewer if asked

- In an awareness test done by the company, the drug had comparable awareness compared to its peers

- Similarly, for distribution, there is adequate penetration in pharmacies relative to competitors
- And, as far as sales force is concerned, this company has 2,000 sales people compared to 1500 for the competitor
- Our sales force covers all the cardiovascular doctors in the country – 300,000 of them, but so do the competitor's sales force.

Solution

Begin by forming a hypothesis and state it to the interviewer, using it as the structure for your response. You can then modify the hypothesis as you receive more information and eventually reach a conclusion.

The problem here is marketing-related, so you can choose any framework appropriate for the situation. One example would be to form the hypothesis that the problem is in one of the following three areas:

- **Awareness** – consumers may not be aware of the product
- **Pricing** – the product may be very expensive
- **Distribution** – the product may not have adequate distribution in pharmacies

Here, you go through each of these three potential causes by asking relevant questions The interviewer provides all the information above, i.e. that awareness is similar, distribution is adequate, and the salesforce is both large and reaches all doctors who prescribe the medicine.

This narrows the problem down to two potential areas: pricing, and the effectiveness of the sales force. The interviewer may tell you that either one of these is the more relevant, and ask you to dive deeper. Let's say here that the interviewer tells you that pricing is not important, as patients are fully insured and thus don't pay themselves for the drug.

Now, you can revise your hypothesis: awareness, pricing, and distribution are probably not significant factors. The sales force also is large enough, but maybe something is not working well in the sales process. You then ask how the sales force is structured. Do they focus exclusively on cardiovascular doctors or is their time distributed on other things as well?

The interviewer tells you that the sales force is responsible for selling all the products of the company, not only Axeles. Thus, only a small proportion of their time goes into marketing the drug, in contrast to the competitor, where the sales force only focuses on selling this one drug.

You can now revise your hypothesis further, stating that this indicates that the effectiveness of interactions between the sales people and cardiovascular doctors is lower than for the competitor.

The interviewer tells you that it sounds like a plausible explanation. To test your creativity, the interviewer asks how this could be measured.

You give some examples, e.g.: frequency of visits, length of each visit, depth of information provided, and ability to answer doctors' technical questions.

The interviewer asks you what you would suggest that the client does now?

You suggest a small-scale test with a few doctors to explore whether the hypothesis of a poor-quality sales force interaction is a reason why they don't prescribe Axeles. Then you suggest to conduct a cost-benefit analysis for having a dedicated salesforce for Axeles.

Case #16: Commercial real estate

Question

Buildbig Inc. is a commercial real estate development company in the United States, operating mainly in the New York metropolitan area. The company has several branches throughout the tri- state area but has most of its business in New York State. Buildbig is owned by the influential Rockgate family and has been in business for decades. The company engages in land acquisition and commercial property development and construction.

1) The management team recently made some rather unsuccessful investments in an attempt to grow Buildbig's business. The CEO is asking you for advice on their future growth strategy. How would you approach the request made by the Buildbig CEO?

2) In order to be less vulnerable to the market forces, the CEO would like to know what her options are. What would be potential ways to achieve this?

Information provided if asked:

- The company's previous investments were heavily influenced by changes in the market place
- Buildbig is still in the same position vs. its competitors as it always was
- The customer base has not changed much
- Internal capabilities are excellent for the commercial building market

Solution

This case tests your ability to think about abstract strategic problems.

For the first question, you should show understanding that this is a market expansion problem and explore the market dynamics:

- **Market**: current size, growth, relative growth in comparison to other U.S. States / other markets / GDP, market stability, market regulation
- **Competition**: who are the competitors, how big are they relative to Buildbig, how strong is competition, are there new entrants, what is their relative growth
- **Customers**: who are the customers of Buildbig, have there been any changes in customer composition and size of the customer base
- **Capabilities**: what is Buildbig good at, what are their key strengths relative to other builders: e.g. relationships, sales & marketing, production, finance, supplier management, etc.

An excellent answer would mention the above plus picking the most relevant answer category and explaining why this category. Any will do, but since the real estate market is very sensitive to the market forces, market size and growth is a good start.

For the second question, the options are to:

- Expand in current market space
- Expand to adjacent geographical markets
- Expand to adjacent segments / product areas
- Any combination of the above

An excellent answer would include an assessment of what the most interesting options are based on real current developments, and explains why one is more attractive than the other.

Case #17: Concrete manufacturer

Question

Your client, a concrete manufacturer is considering acquiring a small local firm. What factors should be considered? After considering these factors, would you recommend the acquisition?

<u>Information to be given if asked:</u>

Margins

- The target firm is currently profitable, with margins of 5%.
- Your client's margin is 15%.
- Your client attributes its higher profit margin to economies of scale in trucking and mixing, and a stable labor force.

Market

- Both companies compete in the geographical market, the South-eastern U.S.

- Your client's customers are large construction firms and contractors generally in the office and commercial
- building construction business.
- The smaller firm sells mainly to other small businesses and contractors. (Swimming pool installation firms, patio builders, etc.)
- Additional research shows that the smaller customers for concrete are growing, while the major office building construction market is stagnant.
- The smaller firm has strong contacts with many local customers, and is often the preferred supplier due to their customer responsiveness.

Financing

- Your client is not able to fund the acquisition internally, but could obtain bank financing at a rate of 10%.
- Similar acquisitions generally are made for two to three times current sales of the target firm.

Solution

This is a two-phased question:

1) What factors should the client consider?

Here, you should use an M&A framework to structure your response. There are many ways to do this, but here is one example:

When considering the acquisition, the client needs to consider factors in four areas: strategic factors, financial factors, industry environment, and cultural feasibility:

Firstly, clarify the strategic effects of the acquisition:

- Does it improve market position,
- Provide growth opportunities,
- Improve sales / distribution,
- Gain new talent or technology?

Secondly, consider financial and operational factors:

- Target's size and revenues
- Target's profitability
- Target's mix of products and customers

- Financing options and cost of capital

Thirdly, assess the industry environment:

- Is the market growing or shrinking?
- Is the industry fragmented or consolidated? Any changes occurring?
- Where is the negotiating power? Do suppliers, buyers, or substitute products have power?
- What drives revenue and profitability growth of firms?

Lastly, evaluate the cultural aspect of an acquisition:

- Would the target be receptive to an acquisition?
- What risks need to be considered? I.e. legal, political, cultural?
- Has the client integrated companies like this successfully before? Is integration realistic?

As you go through this, the interviewer should provide you with the information provided below the question, which you can then use to answer the second question.

2) Would you recommend the acquisition?

From a financial point of view, the acquisition is not attractive if there are no synergies between the firms. With profit margins of only 5%, the income generated by the smaller firm will not cover the capital charges (interest due to the bank) on the acquisition price. (Acquisition price = 3 x sales. Interest on this amount will be 10% x 3 x sales, or 30% of annual sales. Profits are only 5% of sales. This analysis, of course, ignores the tax shields.)

However, if your client were able to use some of its competitive advantages to improve the financial outlook of the target firm, the acquisition would be advisable. It is reasonable to expect that synergies would arise from economies of scale in trucking and mixing, which could raise the profit level of the target firm, and make the acquisition more attractive.

Case #18: Golf balls

Question

You are visiting a client who sells golf balls in the United States. Having had no time to do background research, you sit on the plane wondering what is the annual market size for golf balls in the U.S. and what factors drive demand. Your plane lands in fifteen minutes. How do you go about answering these questions?

Solution

When solving an estimation question like this, break it down into an appropriately detailed framework. If the framework is too simple, you miss an opportunity to demonstrate your abilities. If the framework is too detailed, you will run into problems when going through the mental maths.

Here is an example framework and solution:

The total number of golf balls sold can be broken down into the total number of players, times the number of balls used per player per year:

# of golf balls = (# of golf players) X (# of balls used per player per year)

Let's begin with the first part of this equation. The US-population is 350 million. Let's assume that those between the ages of 20 and 70 are potential players, or about 2/3 of the population. Potential players then, are 230 million. Of these, let's assume that one in ten plays golf regularly, so 23 million regular players.

Now for the second part of the equation. Let's assume that a regular player plays 18 holes two times per week, or 36 holes. If one ball is lost or damaged every 10 holes, the player needs approximately 4 balls per week, or 200 balls per year.

Multiplying 23 million players with 200 balls per year gives us 4.6 billion golf balls sold annually in the United States.

Case #19: Paint

Question

This question was asked by McKinsey in a 1st round interview.

Your client is the CEO of a paint manufacturing company. One McKinsey team has previously worked on optimizing their cost structure. The CEO wants to further improve their profitability. How would you analyze the situation?

Information to be given if asked

Customers

- The customers are of 2 types: professionals (contractors) and private consumers.
- The customers are not very loyal.
- They have multiple brands and have good basic quality paint.

Company

- The total revenues are 1B.
- There are 3 sales channels as follows:
- Company owned stores: 600M in sales. Focuses on contractors (professionals).

- Consumer division: 300M in sales. Sold through mass merchandisers.
- Independent dealers: 100M in sales. Sold to local mom & pop stores. The client maintains a separate set of warehouses to serve this channel.
- Return on sales is 5% for the company owned stores, 3% for the consumer division, and 1% for independent dealers
- The target for the firm is $80M.

Industry

- The industry growth rate is same as GDP growth.
- Client has 30% market share.
- 2nd competitor has 35% market share. There are number of small regional and local paint manufacturers as well which serve the rest of the market.
- The competitors also have 3 distribution channels. There is no data on competitor's profitability.

Solution

This is a profitability question. The first step is to identify the information you need, which the interviewer will provide if you ask the right questions. The second step is to use the information to provide recommendations.

Starting with the first step, we have been told that another team has already optimized the cost structure, so the profitability framework may not be appropriate here. Instead, another way to inspect the problem would be to use a strategic framework to understand the underlying dynamics. One potential framework here would be the 3 C's. Another one would be Porter's Five Forces.

After articulating and going through a framework, asking the key questions in each category, you should have the information available from the interviewer.

Using the channel and return on sales (ROS) information, you can start by calculating the current profitability: 600M * 5% + 300M * 3% + 100M * 1% = 40M. Thus, the target of $80M would mean a doubling of the current profitability.

At this point, you should recognize that the company-owned store channel has the highest ROS (return on sales). One recommendation then would be to focus on this segment. In contrast, the independent dealer channel has the lowest ROS. The client needs to re-evaluate their strategy / presence in that channel.

Another important point is that loyalty is an issue. One way to resolve this is to introduce switching costs. One technique would be order automation by establishing web presence, which will allow the contractors to quickly and easily re-order. Another would be an adjusted service or delivery model to incentivize loyalty.

Thirdly, costs have been optimized, but revenues have not. The client should investigate whether their sales force is effective in selling to the contractors, e.g. by assessing the sales force compensation and commission structure. Another revenue area to inspect would be pricing: perhaps higher prices, combined with better service or higher quality products, would improve profitability for the company-owned stores channel. Contractors in particular may be less price-sensitive, as they often charge their clients for material expenses.

Case #20: Aluminum cans

Question

An aluminum can manufacturer has discovered a way to improve its manufacturing process. As a result, its manufacturing cost has been reduced from $0.89 to $0.79 cents. How can the manufacturer best exploit this cost advantage?

Information to be given if asked

Market

- The client is the leader in its market with a 40% share and supplies directly to major beverage manufacturers.
- The number two player in the market has about 30% of the market and many small competitors share the rest.

Substitutes

- Aluminum cans have a lower priced substitute, steel cans, which have inferior printing and stamping characteristics.
- Steel cans are used by customers who do not want to pay the premium for aluminum cans.

Solution

This solution depends on you having a basic knowledge of microeconomics. Here, the firm can either use the new improvement to implement a penetration strategy or a price skimming strategy. Consider the impact of either strategy on the company and its competitors. Also, don't forget to think about any substitutes for aluminum cans.

Clearly, the client should either drop price or reap additional profits.

If the client drops prices, other competitors will have to follow since this is a commodity market and not following would mean a quick demise. The lowering of prices might increase the client's market share marginally, but some smaller competitors will have to start exiting the industry and larger competitors will have to start investing to discover the client's cost advantage.

At the same time, steel can users will start switching to aluminum cans, thus hurting manufacturers in that market. The resulting growth in the aluminum can market will attract steel can manufacturers to enter it. Since some steel can manufacturers have deep pockets and a strong backing, these new entrants could pose a future threat to our client.

In conclusion, it is best to retain prices and generate extra profits for now. The cost advantage may help another day during a price war.

Case #21: Chicken vitamins

Question

This question was asked by McKinsey in a 1st round interview.

Your client is a US-based chicken vitamin manufacturer. The vitamin helps increase the size of chicken breast and reduce fat content. Should they enter China?

Information to be given if asked

Chicken Industry in China

- Chinese chicken industry is twice as large as US in terms of amount of chicken consumed.
- Growth trends are similar to those of US.

Customers

- The customers in US consist primarily of large corporate farmers e.g. Tyson, Purdue.
- The customers in China can be segmented into 3 categories:

Customer Segment	Current Market Size	Growth (last 5 years)
Family poultry farms	80%	1%
Village farms	10%	19%
Corporate farms	10%	80%

Competition

- There is no direct competitor at the moment in China. There is one substitute product which sells for 47cents/lb.
- The client's product is superior in performance and has no side effects compared to the substitute product.

Firms Resources

- Magnesium is an important ingredient used to manufacture the vitamins.
- The firm has one mine in Florida which is operating at max capacity.
- There are mines in other parts of the world, which have a cost structure as follows (includes transportation of raw material to China)

- 2 in Europe - 39 cents/lb.
- 1 in Africa - 35 cents/lb.
- 1 in India - 37 cents/lb.
- 1 in China - 38 cents/lb.
- Note: These are prices if the client were to acquire the mines.
- Total costs for the rest of the value chain in China (manufacturing, sales & marketing, and distribution) is 10 cents/lb.

Solution

You can use any common business framework to uncover the information you require for this case. When you have done so, the solution is straightforward:

You can begin by drawing a basic value chain for the vitamin manufacturing/distribution process.

Raw Material -> Manufacture vitamin -> Sales and Marketing -> Distribution

For the raw material, choose the mine in Africa, as it has the lowest costs. Adding 10 cents to the price of raw material yields 45 cents/lb. as total cost for the vitamins in China.

You can now make a recommendation. The client should enter China for the following reasons:

- The corporate market is growing rapidly (80% in 5 years). The corporate farms are more likely to use vitamins than the small family farms.
- The client should acquire the mine in Africa
- Total costs are 2 cents lower than the substitute product, and there is no significant competition.

Case #22: Cure for headaches

Question

Your firm just discovered a breakthrough formula for common headaches. What would you do now?

Information to be given if asked:

- You are the CEO of this firm and your firm is a large MNC (multinational corporation).
- The product has passed the first round of in-company testing very successfully.
- We are highly confident that it will be provide the masses instant relief from almost all types of headaches.
- This is a unique discovery, and no existing product comes close to it in terms of effectiveness.
- Almost the same answer to all other questions: "Please make a reasonable assumption." No tables and no graphs

Solution

This case is more open-ended than most, meaning that the specific solution is not what is being tested. Instead, the main purpose here is to assess your ability to think and communicate in a structured manner, make reasonable assumptions, and display your knowledge of frameworks and tools.

You should start your solution by first outlining a high-level picture of what you will assess, which is called "setting the scope" in consulting, and then prove the details of each section, making assumptions and discussing your observations using various frameworks and tools.

One example of setting such a high-level outline is to explore:

- Company's current status
- Impact of new discovery
- Feasibility of product's market success
- Next steps for the firm

Having done something akin to the above, you should be able to proceed on the detailed analysis by leveraging some frameworks like:

- Customer/Competitor/Company (three Cs) analysis
- Internal/ External elements
- Cost revenue and profitability,
- Porter's five forces, etc.

Make necessary assumptions like implications of FDA regulations, patent protection, clinical testing success, and competitor response.

In summary, you need to provide a structure to the problem, flesh out issues with probing analysis and produce a clear next-steps summary for the firm.

Case #23: Water purifier

Question

A leading global consumer goods company has come up with a new product for cleaning water to make it fit for drinking. The product is a sachet which contains a powder. The powder is poured into a bucket of water and stirred for 20 minutes. At the end of the process, the silt/dirt that was in the water will settle at the bottom of the bucket and the bacteria in the water will have been cleaned/neutralized. On pouring, the recipient gets World Health Organization certified drinking water.

The company has launched this product with varying rates of success in many developing countries and now they want to enter India. Your first task is to make a rough estimate of the market size for the product. We know that 1 sachet can be used to clean 10 liters of water.

Solution

Tip:

This is a typical estimation question. You should drive the estimation step-by-step, talking the interviewer through each of your steps and asking the interviewer for information where you need it. If you are uncertain about any of the numbers you are estimating, then validate the number and the assumptions you based it on with the interviewer. It is far better to validate a number with them than use a number that is way out and risk coming up with a nonsensical answer at the end of the estimation as a result. Having said that, you must also demonstrate business judgment and confidence, so don't seek reassurance at every step – only if you need it.

The solution:

You should acknowledge that, given the product can be used to purify 10 liters of water, it will most likely be purchased by households. An example solution would estimate the market size by: 1) estimating the likely market size (in number of households), 2) calculating the average consumption per household (sachets per annum).

1) Number of households

Population of India = 1 billion people

Assume an average 5 people in a household (Indian families are generally bigger than Western families)

Total number of households = 200 million

A sensible hypothesis is that the product will probably be used by households which do not already have access to clean drinking water through basic state-owned infrastructure. These will most likely be households in non-urban areas.

The product will be used by households who do not have the disposable income to purchase easier, less time intensive, alternative sources of purifying water, e.g. filters, bottled water, etc. These will, therefore, be the lower income households.

Given India is a developing country it is fair to assume that a larger percentage of the population will be in non-urban areas. You can use your knowledge of UK (a developed country) where the urban/rural split is probably 70/30. Hence, in

India it might be fair to assume that the split is the reverse – Urban/Rural = 30/70.

Based on this hypothesis, your initial market consists of the rural households = 70% * 200 million = 140 million

Based on your income hypothesis, estimate the income division in the rural areas. Given that the Indian rural economy is mostly agriculture-based and from your knowledge of the high poverty in India, it is also fair to assume that the split between high/low income in rural India is 30/70.

Based on this assumption the initial market size estimate can be improved to 70% * 140 million = 98 million ~ 100 million.

Hence, you can say that the market for this product will consist of 100 million households in India.

Further refinement might include splitting the regions between urban (major cities), semi-urban (towns and the poorer outskirts of major cities), and rural areas (villages), and make their market size estimations on this basis.

Note: You should realize that though there is no proper drinking water infrastructure in villages, water from the wells or rivers is probably cleaner than the stagnant water from the tanks in towns and the outskirts of major cities and that, therefore, in rural areas it is probably fair to assume that perhaps a quarter of the households are happy with, and healthy on, their current water source.

The next step is for you to calculate the drinking water consumed per household and, hence, the number of sachets used per annum:

2) Consumption per household

Assume that 1 household consumes 10 liters of water per day based on fact that 1 person consumes 2 liters per day

Estimation given that in the West we are advised to drink 1.5 liters of water per day for healthy living, and India is in general a hot country

Given that 1 sachet can clean 10 liters of water, 1 household uses 1 sachet per day.

Note: Other factors that you might want to consider are that the drinking water consumption will vary with age of members in a household and on the geographical location of the regions (hot/colder). In general, though, it is fair to mention these points but then take average values.

Note: It is vital for this type of "back of the envelope" estimation not to over-complicate the approach. Keep it simple, then add comments about possible further refinements you might want to consider.

Conclusion

This gives a total of 100 million sachets per day, or 36.5 billion sachets per year.

You should summarize that the target market will consist of people who live in semi-rural and rural areas, and have low income such that they cannot buy the expensive substitutes for the product.

Case #24: Water purifier, continued

Question

This case is a continuation of the previous case, with two new tasks:

1) Having estimated the market size, your next task is to understand the revenues and costs associated with the product. From the company's experience of launching in other developing countries, the average price for the product has been 6.2 US cents. How do you think the product should be priced in India?

2) Also, let's look at the costs of the product. From experience of launching in other countries, the firm knows that the fixed cost of setting up a new manufacturing plant/machinery is 100 million dollars, the variable manufacturing cost is 3.5 cents per sachet, and the other variable costs are 20% of the variable manufacturing costs. What do you think the other variable costs are (i.e., the 20%), and how many sachets does the company need to produce to break even?

Solution

1) Pricing in India

You should use the information discussed in previous questions to come up with a pricing strategy. Price can be determined on a number of different bases, some of which are better than others:

- **Cost plus** – cost of the product plus a margin
- **Price of direct/indirect substitutes** – you should note that all the direct and indirect substitutes discussed before provide different benefits and therefore a different 'value proposition' to the customer. You should assume that the company's aim is to maximize their profit, but that to obtain sizeable market share they need to be priced below the closest, cheapest substitute, i.e., bottled water
- **Customers' willingness to pay** – this can be determined either by primary market research, or by creative means of estimating the percentage of a typical household's disposable income spent on bottled water, or even the health bill related to waterborne diseases

The price for the company's product should, therefore, be such that it covers the product cost but is less than the price of the closest indirect substitute, i.e. bottled water. Note that purely using cost-plus pricing will not work as is takes no account of competitors' pricing or customers' ability or willingness to pay. However, it is worth mentioning it as an option and any product price does need to pitched above the product cost if the company is going to make a profit.

Given that India is quite representative of other developing countries, we can probably use the average price charged in other countries, as long as that meets the criteria we have mentioned above. Hence, it is fair to recommend that the company set a price of 6.2 US cents for their sachet in India.

2) Cost analysis

You should review the value chain post-manufacturing and identify other variable costs. Once the product has been manufactured and packed (assume manufacturing costs includes packaging), then you have to transport the packaged goods from the warehouses to the distribution outlets. In addition to the transportation costs, you will have the sales effort of getting the distributors and the commission paid to the distributors. Hence, to summarize the other variable costs will be:

- Transportation
- Sales
- Commission to distributors

Moving onto the calculation, you should first calculate the total variable costs: VC = 3.5 + 0.2 * 3.5 = 4.2 cents

FC = 100 million

To break even,

Price * Quantity = FC + VC * Quantity

Quantity = 100 million dollars / (6.2 – 4.2) cents = **5 billion sachets**

Hence, the company needs approximately 1/7th (5/36.5) of the market to break even.

Case #25: Pharma growth

Question

Your client is a highly profitable pharmaceutical company that has a world leading position in one therapy area (TA) and is a niche player in a non-related therapy area. The company currently has annual sales growth of 8%, but the CEO has set a target annual growth rate of 12- 15% – in other words s/he wants to triple their revenue over next 10 years.

However, their research project pipeline is thin. The research-and-development organization is heavily under-spending compared to their budget (they have a budget target of around 16% of revenue, but are not using all the money allocated). Senior management has little insight in how the R&D department operates

What is the client's key issue/problem? And what initial suggestions do you have for improving their revenue growth and failings in the R&D department?

Additional information provided if asked:

- A therapy area is a disease area, i.e., oncology, diabetes, respiratory or pain control
- They develop and sell prescription drugs only
- Their growth target is ambitious but not unrealistic (given the money they have for investments and typical industry development)
- Both TAs contribute equal to profit, but the world leading TA generates twice as much revenue as the niche TA

World-leading/ mature TA	Niche TA
Traditional core business of company	Small unique products, highly profitable, but limited demand (not that many people need it)
Mature TA with limited market growth and fairly stable competitive situation	Only sold to specialist and hospitals
Sold via general practitioners	There is some room for expansion of product to other areas

World-leading/ mature TA	Niche TA
Portfolio of products, which has IP protection for 6-8 years	High growth and very competitive TA

Solution

1) What is the client's key issue/problem?

Notes:

- This is an open-ended question to test if you have taken in the information given.
- It is important to realize from the information that revenue is the concern, not profit. Prescription drugs are a highly regulated area and that regulation is in place to ensure that successful product launches typically generate the desired profit margins, without exploiting customers.

Example solution:

The client's issue is that while they are growing at what sounds like a reasonable rate, they are not meeting the annual revenue growth targets that the CEO has set.

They also have a significant problem in their R&D department. As the pharmaceutical industry is very R&D driven (i.e., R&D is necessary to develop new products and there is usually a significant time lag from initial research to product launch), strong R&D is necessary to produce strong revenue growth. The research pipeline is thin and because R&D is under spending it looks like the pipeline will remain thin, unless changes are made in that department.

In addition, senior management do not have a good understanding of the R&D department, which means that they probably do not understand the underlying drivers of the thin pipeline & the under-spending. I would hypothesize from what you've already told me that the problem in R&D (whatever that problem is) is largely responsible for the lower than desired revenue growth.

2) What initial suggestions do you have for improving their revenue growth and failings in the R&D department?

Note:

This question tests your creativity, as well as your ability to give a structured solution with clear recommendations

Example solution:

Because it's a question of revenue, I would like to firstly explore the two levers effecting revenue, which are Price and Quantity (Revenue = price * quantity).

Let's begin with price. You have already told me that the market is highly regulated. Therefore, I would assume that our client does not that have many options to generate significant growth in terms of price.

So, we move on to quantity. There are a number of ways in which our client could potentially increase the quantity of the drugs that they sell:

- Firstly, they could look to expand into new geographical regions
- Interviewer: They are currently in all markets of interest
- Ok, so if geographical expansion is not an option, they could look at trying to increase their market share in their current markets
- There are two ways to achieve this: 1) sell more to existing customers, 2) sell to new customers
- Interviewer: The client is slowly growing their market share in the world leading TA, but it is unlikely that they can grow significantly more. In the niche area, they have unique products with little competition – unless more people

need their products, it is unlikely to see growth

- In that case, their remaining option is to try to increase the overall size of the market, i.e., grow the pie by developing and selling new products to both existing and new customers
- Interviewer: That is correct. New/more products (potentially in new non-related areas) would enable us to grow.

OK, so turning my attention to the failings in the R&D department, you said in your introduction that they have two key problems – firstly, a thin pipeline and under-spending and, secondly, the fact that senior managers do not understand the R&D department, so have probably, historically, been unable to identify the underlying drivers of the under-spending and thin pipeline, and to solve them.

There are a number of reasons they could be under spending:

- Not enough good research projects on which to spend
- Lack of R&D talent
- Lack of motivation/incentives to staff

- Budget control problems

There are a couple of reasons why management has a lack of understanding what is going on:

- Unclear organizational structure
- Lack of useful management control procedures/tools

Case #26: Logging company

Question

You are hired by a Canadian logging company to analyze its current operations and provide advice on future operations. The government regulates the logging industry in Canada. Land is leased to individual companies by the government. The company is making a lot of money and is unsure why. You have been asked to determine: (1) Why they are making money? (2) Is it sustainable? (3) Is it replicable?

Information to be given if asked:

Products

- The company produces lumber boards of two sizes 2"x4" and 2"x8".
- Lumber is a commodity product and as such the company is a price-taker in the market.

Costs

- The government leases tracts of land at an annual price that is set to allow for a 12% profit margin for the entire logging industry.

Thus, all tracts of land have the same lease price per acre.

- The leases last for 99 years and the original lessee has the right of first renewal on the lease.
- The company has a 5% cost advantage in its "tree-to-dock" production process. There is no significant difference between the distribution costs among the industry firms.

Profit/Revenue

- The profit equation for the lumber industry can be written as: Profit per ft3 = Revenue per ft3 - Non-land cost per ft3 - Lease Cost per ft3
- There is a revenue advantage for the company due to its product mix.
- Margins are higher on 2"x8" boards than on 2"x4" boards.
- The company's product mix is made up of a greater percentage of 2"x8" boards than the "typical" logging company percentage.

Production Process

- The cost advantage is not generated by a better logging process (i.e. better equipment, more skilled laborers) but instead exists because of the exceptional quality of the trees on the particular piece of land that the company leases.

- The mineral content of the land leads to faster growth of healthier trees, which improves both yield and turnover. Healthier trees are straighter and easier to cut, thus reducing costs in each phase of the logging process. These healthier, taller, straighter trees yield more 2"x8" board feet than is typical and leads to the advantaged product mix.

- There are no significant economies of scale to the process.

Solution

First, make sure you write down the key points of information, and the three questions you are supposed to answer, before proceeding with the case. You can review these points with the interviewer to ensure you understood everything correctly. Doing this is your responsibility, as the interviewer will not necessarily correct you if you misunderstand something.

Next, use a strategic framework to uncover the information you need (3 Cs would be a potential choice here). Make sure to ask about the things mentioned in the question as you proceed through the structure you have decided upon. They provide you with a hint as to where the keys to solving the case lie. This will be in the form of a conversation with the interviewer, in the same way as you have already seen in previous cases here on Case Ivy. Lastly, after uncovering the information you need, ensure that you give your answer in the same way as the question was framed, using the insights you have gathered:

1) Why they are making money?

The company leases land with a significantly higher quality of trees. This leads to a revenue advantage because more 2″ x8″ board feet can be produced per acre of land. Additionally, there is a cost advantage because the higher quality inputs make the logging process easier and increase yields and turnover.

2) Is it sustainable?

Since the leases are for 99 years and renewable, the current situation seems sustainable.

3) Is it replicable?

Since it is unlikely that another piece of land similar to this one exists or that another firm will give up advantaged land, the situation is not replicable.

Case #27: French fries

Question

How many individual french fries does McDonald's sell in the U.S. each year?

Solution

This is an estimation case. Previously, we have mostly used population/household estimates for these types of questions. However, in this solution, we will estimate the number from the seller's perspective instead of a demographic approach. Often, both approaches can be used, and it is up to you to decide which one is more appropriate.

We first factor the estimate down to components which are easier to estimate:

# of fries sold per year = (# McDonald's restaurants in the US) x (# fries sold per restaurant per year)

Let's begin with the # **of restaurants**. This can also be decomposed:

# of restaurants = (average # per city) x (# cities in the US)

Having travelled to quite a few cities in the US, I feel like the average might be around 10 restaurants. Larger cities can have much more, but smaller cities are more numerous and usually have fewer.

For the cities, I will assume that half of the US population lives in cities, and that the average population is 150-200 thousand. Again, small cities are much more common than large ones, which is the reason for my estimate. This gives me an estimate of $(350M/2)/175k = 1000$ cities

So, I estimate 10,000 restaurants in total.

Now I will estimate the # **of fries per restaurant**. I factor the estimate down to be able to make some quick assumptions:

# of fries per restaurant per year
= # of registers (assumption: 4)
* # of hours open per day (assumption: 8)
* servings of fries sold per register per hour
(assumption: 6)
* # of fries per serving (assumption: 50)
* # of days open per year (assumption: 360)

I can provide my reasons for these assumptions if you would like. If not, I will move on to calculating my estimate, which is:

4 registers X 8 hours per day X 6 servings per hour X 50 fries per serving X 360 days per year X 10k restaurants

$4 \times 8 = 32$

$32 \times 6 = 192 \approx 200$

$200 \times 50 = 10k$

$10k \times 360 = 3.6M$

$3.6M \times 10k = 36$ billion fries sold per year

Case #28: Coffee shop

Question

This question was asked by Bain in a 1st round interview.

A friend asked me if I wanted to buy his coffee shop for $100,000. Do you think I should do it?

Information given by interviewer if asked:

Location: The coffee shop is in Vail, Colorado

Products/Prices:

Cup of coffee, $4.00
Bottled Water, $2.00
Pastries, $3.00

Variable Cost:

All products have a 50% margin

Customers:

The shop serves mostly locals, not tourists, so demand is consistent throughout the year

Other Costs:

Rent   was $500   per   month
Wages (for 2 employees) were $8.00 per hour.
The shop is open 12 hours a day, six days a week

The candidate can assume that the coffee shop
will bring in consistent profits over time.

Solution

This is a valuation question. So, to get the value of
the coffee shop, you first need to calculate the
profitability.

Revenues

Begin by estimating the market size. The
assumptions below are just an example, any
reasonable assumptions would do.

Assume that the coffee shop gets 10 customers per
hour in slow hour and 20 customers per hour in a
busy hour. The first and last 2 hours of the day are
busy hours. So, the coffee shop gets 20×4 + 10×8 =
160 customers/day.

If we assume all the hours as busy hours on
Saturday, then we have 20×12=240 hours on
Saturday.

Number of customers / week = 160 x 5 + 240 x 1 =
1040

Number of customers / year = 1040 x 50 = 50,200

Assume 60% of customers order coffee, 30% order pastry, and 10% order a bottle of water, then the spend is:

50,000 x 60% x 4 + 50,000 x 30% x 3 + 50,000 x 10% x 2 = $175,000

Fixed Costs

Rent = 500 x 12 = $6,000

Wages = $8 x 12 x 6 x 50 = $30,000

We can also make assumptions about utilities and insurance.

Profits

Profits = 175,000 x 50% – 36,000 = $52,500

Assume a 40% tax rate:

Profits after tax = 52,500 x (1-40%) = $31,500

Valuation

If we assume that the coffee shop is in operation indefinitely and we use a 10% WACC, then its value would be:

Value = 31,500 / 10% = $315,000

[This formula is for the present value of a perpetuity. If you are unfamiliar with this formula, read about it so you understand and remember it, as it is commonly used.]

Conclusion

The present value of cash flows is three times the asking price. So, as long as the profits would be consistent for the foreseeable future, it would be profitable to buy the coffee shop. The assumption of perpetual cash flows is optimistic, so a price closer to the present value would be less attractive.

Further analysis could be done on the management experience and the competition to ensure that sales would be consistent.

Case #29: Pay phones

Question

This is a market sizing question from a BCG interview.

How many pay phones are there on the island of Manhattan?

Solution

A logical place to begin your analysis might be to ballpark the number of pay phones on Manhattan street corners. If you think of New York City as a grid of streets, you might guess it is about 300 streets long (north to south) by ten streets wide (east to west), so it has approximately 3,000 intersections. You might then assume there is one pay phone for every two intersections, for a total of about 1,500 pay phones.

If you're feeling really creative, you might subtract the number of intersections that are "invalidated" because they fall in the area of Central Park. Say Central Park is ten blocks long by two blocks wide, or 20 intersections. Using your one-pay-phone-for-every-two-intersections assumption, you would want to subtract ten payphones from the original 1,500.

You might then add to the 1,490 the number of pay phones that might be found in restaurants, hotels, schools, hospitals, and office-building lobbies.

Case #30: Dress shirts

Question

Our client is a large department store chain. The CEO knows that men's dress shirts are much less profitable than the rest of his product lines. He believes that if they were evaluated on a fully loaded basis that they would in fact be unprofitable. He is considering taking action to correct this problem.

What would you want to know to determine whether or not the CEO is correct? What corrective action would you recommend?

Information given by interviewer if asked:

- SG&A includes floor sales staff costs as well as promotional and advertising costs
- Operating Cost mainly comprises cost of maintaining and stocking inventory
- The store can be thought of as similar to Nordstrom's or Macy's
- The phrase "fully loaded" means "including all costs associated with the product"
- The table below will be shared all at once when some information in it is requested

	Men's Dress Shirts	Men's Department
Sales	$1,000	$5,000
Gross margin	25%	35%
SG&A	?	$400
Operating costs	?	$300
Inventory	$150	$1,000
Space allocated to product/department	250 sq. ft.	1,500 sq. ft.

Solution

Your main goal in this case is to logically allocate costs and then determine the appropriate action. Essentially, it is a cost accounting problem. You are given a good deal of leeway to provide logical arguments for your allocations and suggested actions. Below is an example solution.

Operating Costs. Interpolating from the department as a whole would allocate $400 * 1/5 = $60. However, an adjustment could be made based on the inventory numbers, which presumably cause this cost item. For the dress shirts, inventory as % of sales is 15% as opposed to 20% for the department. Thus, we allocate $60 * 15% / 20% = $45 to the dress shirts.

SG&A. Here we will assume that marketing and promotional costs are a significant item. A potential argument here is that shirts are promoted less than other items. Possibly, they are not "features" in ads (usually suits and shoes instead), so a partial allocation could be appropriate here as well.

Additionally, we see that dress shirts take up less space per dollar of revenue in the store than the department as a whole (250 sq. ft. per $1000 for dress shirts vs. 1500 * 1/5 = 300 sq. ft. per $1000 for the department). This also leads us to conclude that SG&A allocation should be lower.

Instead of allocating $300 * 1/5 = $80, we will allocate half of that, or $40, to dress shirts.

Conclusion

Running the numbers after these allocations, we have a gross profit of $1,000 * 25% = $250. Subtracting both cost items yields $250 - $45 - $40 = $165, or a 16.5% net margin. For the department as a whole, the net profit is $5,000 * 35% - $300 - $400 = $1750 - $700 = $1050, or a 21% net margin.

Thus, the dress shirts, while less profitable than the department as a whole, are still profitable for the retailer.

Additionally, dress shirts play an important role in the value proposition for a men's department store. They can be considered a necessity purchase that drives traffic and thus sales of complementary items, such as suits, t-shirts, and ties.

The CEO should perhaps reassess.

Nevertheless, there are still potential opportunities to explore in order to improve the profitability of the dress shirts. This includes adding private label brands, changing vendors, increasing or decreasing the scale of offering, promoting more or less, or adjusting pricing.

Case #31: Software outsourcing

Question

This question was asked by BCG in a 2nd round interview.

A US software company wants to offshore its engineering/designing unit to India, as well as to penetrate into the India software engineering market. Should they do it?

Information provided if asked:

Market Share: the company is the industry leader in the US with close followers chasing behind.

Profitability: declining (unknown reason, but increasing labor costs can be a reasonable assumption).

Capability: strong engineering department in the US.

Cost: R&D is the major cost and Indian engineers are estimated to be 1/4 of the cost of the US engineers with the same technical capability.

Customers

- Company has a strong existing customer base in the US.
- Most of the customers are medium to large companies in the US.
- Customers care about the quality of service but are also considering lowering cost in the long run.
- The most profitable clients are large companies in developed countries where the company already has a strong base.
- The company doesn't have any international presence yet.

Competition

- Key US competitors are all off-shoring in order to lower the cost.
- The growth of the international market is impressive compared to the more mature and stable US market.
- Key competitors are expanding their international business aggressively.
- India is one of the fastest growing international markets as well as the one with the largest market size.

Solution

Since it's a two-fold question, a good solution will start with laying out a clear scope and then gather relevant information to analyze the situation.

BCG is known for their 2x2 matrices, and this would be a good situation to draw one up in order to frame all possible scenarios:

		Off-shoring is critical to access local market	
		Yes	No
Other benefits of off-shoring	Significant	Definitely offshore	Offshore but also find out other critical factors to enter the India market
	Minor	Evaluate the India market independently with market, customer, competition, etc.	Stay in current market and strengthen competitiveness

After using a framework to gather the information you need, you should realize that entering the international market, especially the India market, is critical for the company to both fulfill current customer's emerging needs of cost saving and grow its future business. You should also start to compare the competitive advantages between large US companies off-shoring and local Indian players. One way to do this in a clear way would be a feature comparison table:

	US companies	Indian players
Ability to fulfill customized needs	O	
High quality services	O	
Access to most profitable clients	O	
Cost advantage		O
Local market knowledge		O
Local client / government / supply chain relationships		O
Low legal risks	O	O

After doing this, the conclusion here is a clear "Yes". The situation falls into the upper left corner of the matrix because:

In the long-run, even current customers with the established relationship will need to look for cheaper alternatives. The company can offshore its R&D to lower the cost but still keeps its customer service team in the US to maintain the high service quality.

Although clients in the developed country are more profitable, the actual growth of the market is limited. Developing markets like India might not be as profitable as the US, but with the huge and growing market size, even capturing a small percentage of the market can provide substantial profits. The company might lack knowledge of the Indian market, but its strong customer relationship management skills, large existing customer base, and the understating of unique customer needs can be further leveraged in India.

In addition, hiring local talent or partnering with local companies can help solve the concern of the lack of local knowledge.

The legal risk, as well as the political risk in India, can be considered low.

Case #32: Mall pennies

Question

This question was asked by McKinsey.

How much change would you find on the floor of an average mall?

Solution

This seemingly silly guesstimate is a way to test a candidate's "out-of-the-box" thinking. First, estimate how many stores there are in the average mall – say, 50. Now, how many people enter the average store on the average day? A thousand? So, if there are 50,000 visitors to a mall daily, how many lose change? If one in 50, say, drops money (1,000 people a day), how much is the average loss of change? Most amounts are probably small.

People carry fewer quarters, for example, and are more likely to retrieve them. So, let's say that if a person is equally likely to drop a penny, nickel, or dime, then the average person who loses change loses a nickel. That means there would be $500 worth of change on the average floor. If half of that change has been picked up immediately, that would be $250 worth of change.

Also ask: Is there a fountain in the mall? If a fountain is considered to be the "floor" of the mall, the amount of change would obviously increase.

Case #33: Maldovian coffins

Question

This question was asked by McKinsey in a 1st round interview.

Our client is a coffin maker in the Eastern European country of Maldovia. Up until now, he has been in the business of building high-quality, hand-crafted coffins largely by hand with a skilled labor force. Recently, he has seen a substantial change in his market in recent years and is contemplating the future of his business. What are his strategic alternatives, and which one should he choose?

<u>Information to be given if asked:</u>

Value of business:

- Market size
- Population of Maldovia: 4M
- Population Growth: 0%
- Average Life Expectancy: 75 years
- Age Distribution: assume a flat age distribution (i.e. same number of people at every age)

- **Burial Customs**: 75% of deaths are buried in coffins
- **Price**: Coffins are priced at $5,000 for a hand-made coffin.
- **Costs**: Material accounts for 10% of the direct cost, while labor accounts for the other 90%. COGS is $4,800 per coffin. Fixed costs for the business are $700,000 per year. Assume all assets are fully depreciated and ignore taxes.
- **Competition**: Maldovian Coffins has a 10% market share and a relative market share of about 1 (if asked, you may explain that relative market share is the ratio of the company's market share to that of its nearest competitor.)
- **Market Trends, Regulation, etc.**: Assume that the market is expected to continue as it currently is.

Value of assets:

- **Fixed assets**: Since the firm has been building coffins by hand, the fixed assets are essentially only the land and improvements. These are owned outright by the company.
- Book value (i.e. original purchase price) of Land: $20,000

- Book Value of Improvements: $80,000
- Years Owned: 48
- Avg. Real Estate Appreciation: 6% / year

Solution

Your answer should begin by outlining all three possibilities for the manufacturer:

Option 1: Sell the business to a third party
Option 2: Sell the assets of the company and shut it down
Option 3: Keep operating

The question revolves around deciding which of these three options would be most profitable for the owner.

You should also realize that options 1 and 3 are the same, the value of the business, if sold, should be the same as the value of the business if the owner keeps on operating it.

Let's begin by exploring options 1 and 3. Ask for the relevant information you need, which should result in you having what is provided above.

For the market size, you should quickly realize that every year, 1/75th of the population will turn 76 and therefore (on average) will die. So the total market size is 4M * 1/75 * 3/4 = 40k coffins per year.

For the profits, the company has a contribution margin of $200 per coffin, and sells 40k * 10% = 4k coffins per year. Thus, gross profits are $800k per year. Subtracting fixed costs, annual profits are $100k.

Assuming a discount rate of 10% and perpetual cash flows, the value of the business is $100k / 10% = $1M, regardless of if the owner sells or keeps on operating.

Now explore option 2.

Ask for the value of all of the company's assets, and use the information provided to value them:

Using the "rule of 72," a 6% growth rate will double the investment every 72/6 = 12 years. Since the property was held for 48 years, the current value will be $100k * (2 ^ 4) = $1.6M.

Since the assets ($1.6M) are higher than the value of the discounted cash flows ($1M), then it would make the most sense to liquidate the business and sell the assets.

Case #34: Soft drink six-packs

Question

Your client is a major soft drink company. They have been approached by their bottling company with a proposal to change how six packs will be packaged. Instead of using the standard cardboard boxes that hold individual six packs, the bottling company would like to use a plastic device that holds the six pack together by clinging to the top of each can. Is this a good idea?

Solution

As no information is provided, you are expected to talk about the key considerations in a structured way. Use any appropriate framework. Here is an example solution.

First, divide the potential impact of the change into three areas: 1) cost, 2) revenue/marketing, 3) competitive considerations.

Manufacturing cost

Consider what fixed cost investment, or increased variable costs the bottling company will charge to make this switch. Cardboard is probably more expensive than plastic, right? What about supplier power for these two materials. Any difference? How will the fixed cost investment in plastic production be passed on to our client? All issues that should be considered?

Marketing/revenue impact

Consider who our client's customers are (grocery stores, 7-Elevens, etc.), and what they want. Does the plastic make it easier for them to stock their shelves, or is the standard cardboard better for stacking? What about his customers? Do they want to walk out of the store with plastic or cardboard? Propose some market research, and try to determine whether switching will affect the price you can charge per six-pack or the volume of six packs you will sell. These answers will tell you whether it's a smart thing or not.

Competitive considerations

Is our client a market leader, or a market follower? Has the competition already done this, or will he be doing it in the future? Will make this move gives us a strategic competitive advantage or is it necessary to just keep up, or is not necessary at all? I don't know any of these answers, but these are the areas I told the interviewer I was going to look out. What else might you consider?

Case #35: Hepatitis C

Question

A hospital is your client. They conduct Hepatitis C testing for the local community. The hospital has the following testing information:

In the current population, 10% have Hepatitis C and 90% don't have it

Test result probabilities are the following:

Has it	Test	Percent
+	+	90%
+	−	10%
−	−	60%
−	+	40%

If a test result is positive, what is the probability that the patient actually has Hepatitis C? And can doctors do anything to increase this certainty?

Solution

For the first question, you are expected to know – or figure out how to use – Bayes' Theorem. Draw up a tree with the probabilities, which allows you to calculate the answer using simple multiplication and division:

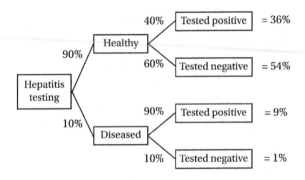

Using the calculated numbers on the right-hand side, you can now find the answer. The probability of having Hepatitis C, given a positive test result, is 9% / (9% + 36%) = 20%

For the second question, you are expected to come up with different alternatives and discuss their merit. Examples include:

- **Run multiple tests**. This would improve the certainty but would probably be expensive

- **Look for other related symptoms.** The doctor could perform a physical if the results are positive, before disclosing the result. This would increase the certainty, likely at a lower cost.
- **Take a complete medical history.** By inspecting the patient's family history and environmental risk factors, their risk of contracting Hepatitis C could be assessed more accurately, also increasing the certainty

Case #36: Diapers

Question

Estimate the size of the disposable diaper market.

Solution

As with other market sizing questions, there are many ways to reach an estimate. The important thing is to use reasonable assumptions, talk through the solution logically, and strike the right balance between detail and rough estimations. Here is an example solution which assumes that the interviewer does not want to spend too much time on this question.

First, I will assume that there are 350 million Americans. I'm going to further assume that the average life expectancy of an American is 80 years. I'm also going to assume that there are even numbers of people in each age group. And that there are exactly same numbers of 8-year-olds as 68-year-olds.

You divide 350 million by 80 and you get about 4.4 million people per age group. Children wear diapers from ago zero to 3 so that's 13.2 million kids wearing diapers. So, we'll round it off to 13 million kids. You said disposable diapers. So, I'll estimate that 90 percent of children wear disposable diapers, as they are more convenient for parents than reusable ones. So now we're talking 12 million children wearing 5 diapers a day. That's 60 million diapers a day times 365 equals approximately 22 billion diapers a year.

Case #37: Airline manufacturing

Question

This question was asked by A.T. Kearney.

In the 1970's, Lockheed Martin manufactured L-1011 wide-body aircraft for commercial airlines. The industry was very cyclical with swings in demand occurring a frequently as every 6 months (see chart below). During the down months, the Lockheed would have to lay off employees and shutter the plants, which created turmoil for the company and the local community. Jet aircraft were normally built to the order specification of the purchasing airline. To alleviate the costs of cyclical swings, Lockheed considered building aircraft to a predetermined schedule based on average expected aircraft sales over the next five years (see image).

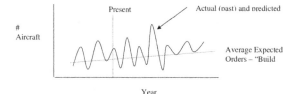

Do you think this is a good idea? What are the pros and cons of pursuing such a plan?

Solution

Unlike some other cases, this case doesn't really have a yes/no solution. The important thing in a case like this is to identify the major issues and state your approach for arriving at a solution. The interviewer wants to see if you have a basic understanding of manufacturing business and the costs inherent in running such an operation. On a real problem like this, you would need to model the costs (with a spreadsheet) of the current (build to order) approach and the new approach (build to schedule) and then test the new approach under a range of sensitivities, both positive and negative. Revenues are unlikely to be impacted by this decision unless having aircraft in inventory would facilitate greater sales.

Example solution:

A good case solution would identify the cost drivers and risks and arrives at an educated guess of the right answer. Let's look at some of the costs and how they would be impacted by a build to schedule plan:

Inventory or Working Capital Holding Costs

This could be huge under a build schedule. If demand is not as predicted or the market heads into a cyclical dip, Lockheed could end holding a lot of very expensive (tens of millions of dollars) of inventory that just sits on the books. At a 6-8% risk-free rate of return, the inventory holding costs of such expensive assets would add up rapidly.

Labor Costs

Labor would probably be cheaper under a build schedule. The company could avoid costly retraining and rehiring of its workforce after the layoff. Additionally, the company would have to pay fewer severance costs due to fewer layoffs. With a more guaranteed production schedule, the company may be able to extract wage concessions from its unions. But, such savings would evaporate if the company were to busily build new aircraft that the market doesn't want.

Technological Obsolescence

With build to schedule, you run the risk of building aircraft that aren't demanded in the marketplace because they are obsolete. Thus, if a competitor introduces a much better model at the existing price points or a technology change renders current models as inefficient, Lockheed would have to liquidate any existing inventory at fire-sale prices.

Forecasting

A build to schedule plan for such costly goods requires a very accurate forecast of future demand. Can demand really be forecasted with sufficient accuracy?

Rework Costs

Airlines request specialized configurations of the aircraft to meet their particular needs. If the company pursues build schedule, they would need to budget rework costs to change pre-built models to the specifications of the purchasing airline. Or, if they only build aircraft partially, how will they handle the production backlog of moving these partially completed aircraft through the remaining production steps?

Fixed Production Equipment and Facilities

In general, the fixed costs of production equipment and facilities should not change with a change in production approach. Now, if the company amortizes equipment on a per unit basis (vice yearly), then net income could be affected under the new plan. But, cash flows, the important thing to look at when making business decisions, should not be affected.

Variable Materials Costs

These include materials and components required for building the aircraft. Under a build to schedule plan, Lockheed could probably negotiate lower costs from their suppliers since they would be able to guarantee a steady stream of purchases.

Unused capacity

Under build to schedule, you're likely to have unused production capacity since you currently carry sufficient capacity to meet cyclical demand surges. The analysis should carefully examine the existing production assets to determine if savings could be realized through capacity reduction.

After identifying the variables, the interview would expect you take a guess on the right answer based on your assumptions. It turns out that build schedule approach is not viable for this company because they cannot predict demand with sufficient accuracy and the capital holding costs are too expensive.

Case #38: Eye drops

Question

You have worked as a McKinsey associate for two years and have recently become an engagement manager. As you complete your preparation for a progress review, a former client calls you needing immediate help.

The client, a marketing vice-president of a major pharmaceutical firm, is working on a business plan for a new revolutionary product. The client quickly explains that their researchers have developed eyedrops which completely eliminate nearsightedness in 60% of the cases (the cases caused by eye strain rather than irregularly shaped eye lenses) if the drops are used twice a day.

The client needs to complete his baseline business plan within an hour so that he can share it with the management committee later that afternoon, but is having a difficult time with two parts of the plan:

First, the client needs a directional estimate of the retail price they should set for the drops so that he can complete the business plan. How would you

help the client structure his thinking on the price
and what is your back-of-the-envelope estimate
on the price that he should use?

Second, the business plan is also missing a
ballpark estimate of the market for the product.
Specifically, what dollar level of sales might he be
able to expect per year in the long run in the US
market?

Solution

Divide your solution clearly into two parts, answering in the same order as was asked:

Part 1: Pricing

The client needs thoughtful pricing insights which provide him with a reference point to choose a price estimate for the eye drops.

One rough cut pricing analysis would determine the market price for the product that is being replaced...in this case, eyeglasses or contact lenses. For example, if eyeglasses cost $120 and last on average 2 years, then a two-year supply of drops could be sold for $120.

A more advanced analysis might determine that eyedrops are simple to use and completely trouble-free so that they should replace the most expensive option including all the costs associated with that option. For example, this may include $100 per year in optometrist fees, $180 in contact lenses ($120 per pair plus on average each user loses on lens in a year), and $25 in contact lens cleaning solutions and other supplies, for a grand total of $305. Using this example, the retail price of the one-year supply of drops should sell for $305.

The most advanced issue trees will include the fact that this new product is actually much better than the alternatives, issues of dynamic pricing strategies (e.g. start high and reduce over time to best understand elasticities), and pricing so that marginal revenue equals marginal cost.

Considering these different possibilities, you end up recommending to the client to use $200 per year as a price estimate. This seems like a good number to use to assess the business case, given the different estimates of $120/2y and $305/y from two of the approaches.

Part 2: Market size

The client also asked you for a quick estimate which market size should be used.

Because you have already determined a reasonable price, you must now estimate the number of yearly supplies that the client can expect to sell in the US. One possible organizing structure (with estimates) is:

Estimate the number of people in the US: 350 million

Estimate the percentage of (1) using corrective eyewear: 20%

Estimate the percentage of (2) that are nearsighted: 70%

Use the client's figure for the percentage of (3) that can be helped: 60%

Estimate the percentage of people that will adopt the new product: 50%

Put it all together: (350 million)(.2)(.7)(.6)(.5) = 14.7 million people

Multiply be the price per unit (14.7 million)($200 per unit) = $2.9 billion

Make sure to mention that this assumes a proprietary product with no competition. If a competitor is assumed, market share must also be considered.

Case #39: Retail bank

Question

This question was asked by Accenture in a 2nd round interview.

Our client is the private division of a retail bank that has 100,000 clients, $500,000,000 in revenues, and $150,000,000 in net income. Our client's goal is to double the revenues and profits of the business in 5 years. Assess the feasibility of the goal. Prioritize the two or three most important steps they should take in their action plan.

Information provided with interviewer if asked:

Pricing: they make their revenues from interest and fees

Costs: transaction costs, salaries. The nature of the sale is one-on-one pitch between the bank salesperson and the customer. So the salary cost and the transaction costs tend to be high.

Geography: They have a large presence in the North East and a moderate presence in the South East

Products: They have 4 product lines, with the following ranks in revenue and profit generation:

Volume	Revenues	Profits
Private banking (deposits, loans)	#1	#1
Investment management (brokerage, advice, access)	#2	#4
Trust (state planning and trust, transferred death)	#3	#2-3
Insurance	#4	#2-3

Customers: 20-25% of customers purchase more than one product. 75-80%% of customers purchase only one product. They are segmented into 5 groups:

Volume	Net Worth	% of Revenues
Ultra High	$10M+	5%
High Net	$1M-$10M	10%
Affluent	$0.5M-$1M	20%
Mass Affluent	$100k-$500k	25%
Mass	$0-$100k	40%

The Ultra High, High Net, and Affluent segments generate 60-70% of the revenues, while the Mass Affluent and Mass segments generate 30-40% of the revenues.

Solution

As before, first confirm with the interviewer that you understood the problem and the supplied information correctly. Then, use an appropriate framework to ask the questions you need to discover the available information (3Cs would be appropriate here, for example). Then proceed to the analysis:

Buyer selection: Since transaction costs tend to be the same for the different customer segments, it makes sense to grow the number of the higher revenue generating customers and decrease the number of the lower revenue generating customers. We can attract the top 3 segments by marketing more selectively and doing promotions for higher income customer groups. We can discourage less affluent customers by raising the prices on them, giving them the option to add more profits or switch to a competitor.

Cross-sell: Since 75% of customers purchase only one product. There's an opportunity for cross-selling between the different product lines. Assuming that we will only serve the top 3 customer segments:

- Revenue generated by customers in top 3 customer segments = \$500M x 70% = \$350M
- Revenue generated by customers who only have one product = \$350M x 75% = \$262.5M

If we assume that the 4 types of products generate comparable revenues, then if we cross-sell each customer 3 other products then the new revenue will be = \$262.5 x 4 = \$1,050M

Conclusion: It is feasible to double revenues and profits if we can only cross-sell our current customers the other products in our business. The next steps Private Retail Bank should take are:

- Give incentives to the bank's sales force to cross-sell different products to its existing customers
- Do promotions for the top 3 affluent market segments
- Increase its prices in its bottom 2 mass market segments to "fire" its unprofitable market segments

Case #40: Distilled spirits

Question

You are consulting for a major United States producer of distilled spirits. Their primary products are a line of mid- priced vodkas and two brands of mid-range rum. Over the past few years, the business has become less and less profitable. What are the possible causes?

Information to be given if asked:

Product

- The split of product sold has consistently been 60% vodka / 40% run over the past few years.
- The selling prices of the two lines are essentially the same.
- Overall sales are growing at about 3 to 5% per year, the same as the industry average for these product lines.

Cost

- Production Costs have remained constant
- Advertising Costs have remained constant on average

- Distribution Costs have increased significantly

Distribution

- The products are sold throughout the country.
- In 27 "open" states, alcohol is sold in privately managed supermarkets and liquor stores. In "open" states, shelf space is extremely expensive and trade promotions are critical. Such stores are also becoming less and less willing to hold inventory, which is increasing distribution costs by requiring more frequent deliveries.
- In the other 23 "closed" states, liquor is only sold through state regulated liquor stores. Distribution costs in these states is much lower, as there are far fewer outlets to service and central warehouses for the state-run stores. Also, Advertising of alcohol is much more tightly regulated, and therefore, advertising spending is lower.

Solution

The solution to this case is straightforward if you manage to ask about the right information. Specifically, your framework needs to touch upon the distribution of the product. Here is an example solution, after receiving the info:

A greater and greater share of the volume is being sold in the "open" states, with sales in these states increasing at about 10% per year. Sales in the regulated states are actually decreasing. Because the regulated states are less expensive to serve, and therefore, more profitable, the fact that they represent a shrinking portion of the total has caused total profits to decline.

Case #41: Gas retailing

Question

For the past thirty years the national government has set the retail price of gasoline for cars. Under a new market reform program, the government has decided to allow the gasoline distribution companies to determine the retail price of gasoline for cars. The CEO of Iberia Gasoline has hired us to advise her on an appropriate strategy for pricing in the country. What would be your recommended price on the first day of deregulation and your ongoing pricing strategy?

Information to be given if asked

Current Situation and Process

- The Ministry of Transportation previously changed the price weekly to assure that the distribution companies make €.10 per litter in gross profit.
- Gasoline is refined to three levels Supra, High and Regular that refers to the level of octane and the degree to which the fuel is unleaded. All firms sell in proportion of 40%, 30% and 30% at the prices of €1.75, 1.60 and 1.50 per

litter respectively, with the same gross profit
(€.10).
- In a deregulated environment, firms have the
capacity to change prices hourly at any
service station based on the pricing strategy.

Consumers and Growth

- Consumers are price *in*elastic across a broad
range of prices, but do go to service stations
based on price, convenience and ancillary
services.
- Currently gasoline sales have been growing
5% per annum as more people live in suburbs
and commute by car to work.

Competitive Analysis

- Currently there are three companies that have
95% market share. Iberia Gasoline has 45%
market share, whilst the remaining two firms
have 25%.
- Iberia's market share is consistent throughout
the country with no one firm dominating one
region or city.
- Each firm solely distributes gasoline; no firm
is involved in oil exploration, extraction or

refining. Consequently, all firms pay essentially the same amount for refined gasoline which they then brand, distribute and sell.

Government Regulations

- Currently the Ministry of Transportation will not allow gasoline retailers to vertically integrate into other areas of gasoline distribution.

Extra Credit

In addition, to gasoline retail gasoline sales the firms also engage in retail activities by co-locating mini-markets in the gas stations that sell items such as soda, cigarettes, snack food, etc. Industry research shows that this area has been the fastest area of growth (10% p.a.) for the firms and nets (25%). However, Iberia Gasoline has been growing at 15% and nets 30% due in part to its superior selection and perception that it is a price leader.

Data provided

The following table is provided if the candidate asks about any of the information in it:

Impact on Gas Sales			Today			
Price	150	155	160	165	170	175
Volume	104	102	100	98	95	75
Revenue	15600	15810	16000	16170	16150	13125
Total Cost (150)	15600	15300	15000	14700	14250	11250
Net Profit	*0*	*510*	*1000*	*1470*	**1900**	*1875*
Impact on Retail Franchise						
Number of Cars	14	12	10	8	6	4
Retail Sales per Car	1000	1000	1000	1000	1000	1000
Gross Revenue	14000	12000	10000	8000	6000	4000
Net Margins	30%	30%	30%	30%	30%	30%
Net Profits	***4200***	*3600*	*3000*	*2400*	*1800*	*1200*
Total Profit	**4200**	**4110**	**4000**	**3870**	**3700**	**3075**

Solution

After getting the information you need, you are supposed to demonstrate an understanding of three key things: the revenue curve with regards to volumes, the impact of retailing on overall profit growth, and the interrelations between gasoline sales, retailing and overall profits.

There are two key areas to consider.

- Firstly, recognize that retail gross margins on gasoline range between 5.8% and 6.8%, with net margins apt to be under 2%, well below what most companies want to earn therefore so price increases are in order. As a market leader, Iberia should clearly signal that they want to raise prices. The firm should actively change prices to maximize yield on their service stations as competitors change their prices. At this point the interviewer should provide different volumes-price scenarios for interviewee to calculate profit-maximizing price (give the above Table to the interviewee).
- Secondly, the gross profits are the same across products. Iberia should explore if all segments are equally price sensitive. Finally

(for extra credit), firms are making most of their money in the convenience stores so driving car volume through the station is key.

An example summary solution would be as follows:

Margins on gasoline erode shareholder capital and should therefore be raised to provide adequate returns. Competitors face the same costs and will follow suite. If we're wrong we can always lower prices and lose little. If we don't take a price leadership then we may permanently lose the chance to do so later. The upside of this strategy is high, whilst the downside risk is low.

Case #42: Consulting firm

Question

You are the managing director of a large international consulting firm. Traditional strengths of your firm have been solving strategy and organizational issues. Recently, you have noticed an increasing number of your firm's proposals are being rejected because of a lack of information technology expertise in your firm. So far, your firm's growth has been strong enough that proposals lost have not hurt annual earnings. Nonetheless, you are becoming increasingly concerned about the need to develop the firm's capabilities in information technology.

Q1: Assuming your concern is valid, what reasons will you provide to other partners about the need to acquire information technology skills?

Q2: Assuming you are able to convince other partners of the importance of IT expertise, what steps would you take to rapidly build IT capacity in this area?

Q3: What are the major risks in executing an IT capacity-expansion?

Solution

Question 1

Good answers focus on the value of IT to clients: discussion topics include the increasing importance of information in business, strategic value of information and information flows, importance of information systems for implementing new organizational structures and management control systems.

Better answers focus on the costs of losing clients to competitors: discussions included the encroachment costs of having clients talking with competitors about IT problems, risk of losing credibility with clients by not being able to solve a problem.

Question 2

Good answers will focus on various methods to build expertise: buying expertise by acquiring another firm, by raiding IT practices of other firms for a few key consultants, building capacity through recruitment of IT experts and training them to be consultants, building capacity by training current consultants in IT practice skills, establishing a strategic alliance with a IT boutique firm.

Candidates should discuss the pros and cons of each method proposed; impact on firm's current culture, cost to the firm, time needed to build expertise, etc.

Better answers will realize the importance of stimulating client demand as capacity builds through seminars, articles strategic studies in IT areas, etc.

Question 3

Good answers depend on the expansion methods discussed, but an important issue is the loss of the firm's focus away from just strategy and organization.

Better answers will focus on the difficulty of implementation in IT; rapid technological changes in the IT industry require significant ongoing training and development costs; new practice cultures may be significantly different from current culture, especially if "external experts" are brought into the organization.

Case #43: Red clothes

Question

How many people wear red in New York City on a typical Monday?

Solution

As with previous market sizing questions, the specific numbers are less important than being organized, making reasonable assumptions and being confident in your mental math.

Make sure to (1) clarify the question, (2) break the problems into smaller pieces, (3) use estimation and judgement to solve each piece, and then (4) consolidate all of those pieces into a final conclusion.

Here is an example solution:

Ok, so here is how I would want to solve this problem. The number of people wearing red in NYC on a typical Monday will be determined by these following factors:

- How many people are there in NY?
- What are chances that people will wear red? This depends on two smaller factors:
- How many pieces of clothes people wear
- People preference in color

Now I will estimate each of those elements:

- Population is about 20 million

- Chances:
- 5% staying at home, 70% going out once, 25% going out twice
- Those staying at home wear 2 pieces of clothes (pants and shirt), those going out once wear 5 pieces (shoes, pants, shirt, scarf/sweater, jacket), and those going out twice will therefore wear 10 pieces
- There is no specific preference on color. I will assume that 10% of garments are red in color.

Now I will analyze the number of people wearing red at each group. I am aware that the probability calculations are not mathematically accurate, but they are good enough for a rough estimate.

1) **Staying at home**:

- 1,000,000 people
- 2 pieces of clothes
- Chance of wearing red in each piece: 10%

1,000,000 * 2 * 10% = 200,000 people

2) Going out once: On a Monday, most will be going to work, so I will assume only a 5% chance of red for each garment:

14,000,000 * 5 * 5% = 3,500,000 people

3) Going out twice: Here the first trip is for work (5% chance) and the second trip casual (10% chance of red), i.e. 7.5% chance of red for the day:

5,000,000 * 10 * 7.5% = 3,750,000 people

So in total: there are about **7.5 million** people in NYC wearing red on a typical Monday.

Case #44: Home security

Question

This is a broad, qualitative strategy case and was given in a very open and conversational manner. No hard data was provided – instead, the interviewer asked the candidate to come up with assumptions and estimates to drive the case forward. Therefore, there is no "right" answer, but the candidate must be able to come up with reasonable assumptions and then follow them logically to a conclusion.

Verizon is the nation's largest provider of local telephone services. They are considering entering the home security market. Should they?

Solution

For an open-ended case like this, you should immediately impose some structure so you can solve it in an organized manner. A good split here would be information gathering first, and recommendation second.

<u>Information gathering</u>

Use a strategic framework you are comfortable with, discussing the themes which will affect your recommendation. Try to cover all of the following subjects:

Market Size: As no info is provided, you need to assess the market size. A sample calculation based on sample assumptions follows:

- Total Households in the US: 100M
- % Households Serviced by Verizon: 50%
- % Households That Can Afford Service: 50%
- Annual Subscription Price: $250
- Total Addressable Market: 100M x 50% x 50% x $250 = $6.25B

Cost Structure: Discuss the fixed vs variable costs, and whether Verizon has an advantage over other players.

The business has the very little fixed cost beyond the infrastructure already installed in potential customers' homes (i.e. the existing phone wiring). Customer would need door/window/motion sensors installed, which could be done by a third-party installer and billed to the customer at cost + markup and owned by the customer.

Variable costs are also very small – essentially just the cost to maintain enough call center operators to dispatch police when alarms are tripped.

Verizon does not seem to have much or a cost advantage over other players since they are all using the common carrier phone network. Verizon might have some economies of scale in operating the call center, but this effect would be slight.

Competition: The market is composed of a large number of mom-and-pop alarm company operators. No firm has over 5% market share overall, although there are some strong regional players.

Customer Segments: We can reasonably divide the customer base into urban and suburban customers, having different needs and different price sensitivities. Urban customers are likely to have lower incomes but a high willingness to pay due to the increased crime rate of the city. Suburban customers are likely to have a higher income but a lower perceived threat due to a lower suburban crime rate. By first-degree price discrimination, it may be reasonable to charge the suburban customers a higher price because they are presumably less price sensitive. We can assume that 50% of customers are urban and 50% suburban.

Pricing: Areas to consider:

- Insurance companies generally give breaks on homeowner's insurance for having an alarm. This will increase the EVA to the customer and can inform pricing.
- What other services to homeowners pay for monthly? Cable, phone, DSL. How are the values of these services perceived compared to the value of the alarm?
- Pricing will need to be competitive with other market players.
- The candidate might assume a net margin based on the competitive landscape and use this with assumed market size to determine attractiveness rather than determining an end-consumer price.

Marketing: Points to identify include:

- Verizon has monthly customer contact with a large pool of potential alarm services customers through its phone bills.
- Verizon already has brand loyalty for phone service, why not alarm service?
- The sheer size of the company (and deep pockets) make it more able to achieve scale economies in marketing and reach a broad audience.

Conclusion

Having discussed the themes above, you then move on to making your recommendation:

So, should Verizon enter the home security market?

Yes. Verizon possesses several small but important competitive advantages for entering into this new market. It has economies of scale in call center operations that will enable it to be highly cost-competitive in operating a security network. It has an established brand that the consumer associates with reliability as well as with networking and communications – the primary function of a home security system. More importantly, Verizon already reaches 50M households every month through its phone services bill that it could leverage to launch and market this new service. Also, the company has deep pockets and the ability to advertise such a service far more effectively than the small, regional competitors.

The size of the opportunity is large enough for Verizon to consider. Assuming a potential market size of $6B in Verizon's territory, even at only a 10% share, Verizon can add $600M in revenue. Given the low-cost structure of this business and the high perceived value to the customer, this is likely to be highly profitable revenue as well. With Verizon's marketing clout and customer reach, the company should be able to gain significant market share and become the national leader in this space.

Case #45: Clock, fire fighter, onions

Question

Sometimes, consulting interviewers skips a market sizing/guesstimate question and instead give you a few, shorter, logic questions. The idea is to test your intellectual capabilities, as these types of questions are more difficult to prepare for. Nevertheless, having experience with the format will make you more comfortable with them, allowing you to focus on the problem at hand. As each of these questions is short, they are combined in batches of three.

1. At 3:15, how many degrees there between the two hands of a clock?

2. A fire fighter has to get to a burning building as quickly as he can. There are three paths that he can take. He can take his fire engine over a large hill (5 miles) at 10 miles per hour. He can take his fire engine through a windy road (7 miles) at 9 miles per hour. Or he can drive his fire engine along a dirt road which is 8 miles at 12 miles per hour. Which way should he choose?

3. You spend 21 dollars on vegetables at the store. You buy carrots, onions and celery. The celery cost half the cost of the onions. The onions cost half of the cost of the carrots. How much did the onions cost?

Solution

1. Clock

If you thought the answer was zero degrees, you'd be incorrect. At 3:15, the clock's minute hand will be pointing at 15 minutes, exactly 90 degrees clockwise from vertical. At 3:15, the clock's hour hand will exactly one quarter of the distance between 3 O'clock and 4 O'clock. Each of the 12 hours on the clock represents 30 degrees (360 degrees divided by the 12 hours on the clock). Consequently, one quarter of an hour is exactly 7.5 degrees, so at 3:15 the minute hand will be at 97.5 degrees. So, there is a difference of **7.5 degrees** between the hour hand and minute hand at 3:15.

2. Fire Fighter

Driving his fire engine 5 miles at 8 miles per hour takes 37.5 minutes. Driving his fire engine 7 miles at 9 miles per hour takes about 47 minutes. Driving his fire engine 8 miles at 12 miles per hour takes 40 minutes. So, he should choose to drive his fire engine **over the hill**.

3. Onions

Answering this problem just requires some simple algebra. If we assume the cost of celery = x, then the cost of onions = 2x, and cost of the carrots is 4x, such that the total cost of all vegetables = x + 2x + 4x = 7x = 21 dollars. Consequently, x = 3 dollars. Hence, the onions cost 6 dollars.

Case #46: Piano, manholes, subway

Question

1. You spend a third of all the money you have on a piano. Half of your remaining money you use to buy a piano chair. A quarter of the rest of your money you use to buy piano books. What proportion of your original money is remaining?

2. Why are manhole cover always round, instead of square?

3. In the Chicago subway system there are two escalators for going up but only one for going down to the subway. Why is that?

Solution

1. Piano

You spend a third of all the money you have on a piano, so you're left with two thirds (2/3). You spend half (1/2) of the remaining two thirds on a piano chair, which leaves you with just one third of what you started with (1/2x2/3=1/3). You spend a quarter (1/4) of what you have remaining (1/3) on piano books, which leaves you with one twelfth of the original (1/4x1/3=1/12).

2. Manhole Cover

A square manhole cover can be dropped down the hole if turned diagonally to the hole, where round covers can't be dropped down manholes.

3. Chicago Subway

People coming into the subway tend to arrive at different times, so the flow of people down the escalators is a more even stream. Conversely, when people get off the subway they typically all arrive at the escalators at about the same time. Consequently, two escalators are need to handle people leaving the subway, where only one is required for people arriving.

Case #47: Boxes, wheat, rugby

Question

1. You find three boxes at the store. One contains onions. Another contains potatoes. The third contains both onions and potatoes. However, all three of the boxes are labeled incorrectly so it's impossible to tell which box contains what. By opening just one box (but without looking in) and removing either a potato or onion, how can you immediately label the contents of all the boxes?

2. There are 8 bags of wheat, 7 of which weigh the same amount. However, there is one that weighs less than the others. You are given a balance scale used for weighing. In less than three steps, figure out which bag weighs less than the rest.

3. There are 23 rugby teams playing in a tournament. What is the least number of games that must be played to find a tournament winner?

Solution

1. Three Boxes

Just open the box that is labeled "Onions and Potatoes". Since none of the boxes are labeled correctly, this box must contain only onions, or only potatoes. If you remove a potato from this box, the box must be the "Potatoes Only" box.

One of the remaining two box has to be the "Onions Only" box. However, the only you currently have it labeled "Potatoes Only", and the other is label "Onions Only". So the box labeled "Potatoes Only" must be the box that contains only onions, and the box labeled "Onions Only" must be the box that has both potatoes and onions.

2. Bags of Wheat

Immediately, take any 2 of the bags and place them to the side. Weigh 3 of the remaining six bags against the other 3 bags. If these bags weigh the same, that means the bag that weighs less must be one of the two that you immediately placed to one side. If this is the case, weigh the 2 bags you placed to one side against each other to find out which one weighs less. You've now found in your bag.

However, upon weighing the sets of 3 bags against one another you find that one set weighs more than the other set, place one of the bags from the set of heavier bags aside and weigh the remaining two bags to find out which one is heavier. If they are of equal weight, the you know that the bag you place to one side is the bag you're looking for.

3. Rugby Tournament

In a tournament, every rugby team except the winner is eliminated from the tournament after being defeated just once. Hence, the number of games required to find a tournament winner is going to be one less than the number of teams, or 22 in this case.

Case #48: Plants

Question

Our client is one of three players in a commodity industry. There are six manufacturing plants operating in this industry. Two belong to our client, two each belong to the other players. One of our client's plants is profitable, one is not. Both are operating at better than 80 percent capacity. Of the other plants in the industry, all but one are profitable.

Without trying to "crack" the case — no competitive analysis necessary — what do you think our client might do to increase profitability?

Solution

In this mini-case, you are expected to demonstrate your ability to use microeconomic principles to deliver a strategic recommendation. Below is an example solution.

Knowing what we know about commodity industries, we should suspect that unprofitable plants mean too much manufacturing capacity.

We cannot control the other plants but we can control our own. I would want to study the scenario of shutting down our unprofitable plant in conjunction with skimming our most profitable customers and shifting them to the remaining plant. This should eliminate our cash sump while raising the price of the commodity (lower supply and same demand now clear at a higher price). Meanwhile, we can focus on the most profitable customers and, as an added bonus, we will have a plant in mothballs as a credible threat against new entrants thinking of joining the fun at a new, higher price.

Case #49: Health clubs

Question

Our client runs a major chain of health clubs in the UK, alongside hotels and casinos (which are not the focus of this case). The health clubs are large out-of-town sports centers offering a gym, Jacuzzi, swimming pool, etc. They are relatively expensive, about £30-40 per month for an individual membership.

As part of a broader strategy review, the client wants to know what they should do with their leisure clubs division – should they sell it, rapidly build more clubs (if so, what sort), or maybe acquire another player? Your specific task on this case is to look at the market trends and assess competition in the leisure clubs industry.

The first key question is – what factors might you analyze to determine what is going to happen to demand for leisure clubs? (In consulting terminology, we are looking at the 'drivers' of demand in the industry)

Solution

This case tests your creativity and ability to think in terms of strategically relevant factors. A good answer will name some of the following factors, with some discussion of the associated issues:

- **Trends in society towards more or less participation in sport** – whilst more participation in sport generally may be positive for demand, increases in popularity of sports not offered at health clubs may have a negative effect (e.g. people may play football instead of going to the gym).
- **Trends in obesity** - if the population is getting more obese, there are two possible implications of this. One is that people are getting more obese because they are not exercising (i.e. declining demand for leisure clubs). The alternative interpretation is that an increasingly obese population will create demand for facilities to exercise more,
- **Trends in available leisure time and money**. If people have more spare time, they are likely to use health clubs more.
- **National income / state of the economy** – leisure clubs are likely to be a luxury good, for

which demand will decline if there is a
recession.

- **Demographics** – younger people are more
  likely to be members of gyms. Therefore, if the
  population as a whole is getting older,
  demand for leisure clubs is likely to decline

An excellent answer will name most of the above
factors, with more explanation of why they are
important, and may include other sensible
suggestions e.g. "sales of Slim Fast would be a
good indicator of what has been happening to
demand for leisure clubs, because people who
buy Slim Fast are the type of people who would
use leisure clubs".

An excellent candidate will also be able to defend
sensible answers when questioned or pushed on
why a particular factor is important; often it is at
this point in the case study where excellent
candidates differentiate themselves.

Case #50: Wireless launch

Question

It's 2:30 a.m. and you are finalizing some last details to launch a new wireless telecommunication service in the smallest market of seven in Austria. For the client, Austria Star Mobile (ASM), it will be their first launch of seven potential launches in Austria and they want it to be a flawless and successful in order to raise capital. Your team has just finalized the pricing strategy and ordered 100,000 pieces of promotional material when you get a call from the CEO of Austria Star. The CEO says he was just at conference in Singapore with the president of the incumbent wireless provider, AT& M, who says that they will beat the price of any new entrant in Austria by 10%. The CEO of Austria Star wants to know how they should respond to this news. What do you do?

Information to be given if asked:

Current Industry Structure/Market share

- AT&M currently controls 100% of the entire Austrian market for mobile and landlines and 30% of the cable television market and operates extremely profitably with all these products.

- Two other mobile providers will enter the market 6 months after Austria Star.
- The market is growing at 20% p.a.

Competitive Information

- AT&M is known to have thorough coverage of Austria, but is known for busy lines, dropped calls, and haphazard service.
- AT&M's rates are a flat €10 per month plus €.40 per minute, or flat €30 per month and €.20 per minute, flat €60 per month and €.10 per minute.
- Your team has spent the last three months developing a highly flexible pricing model. The model suggests that the optimum rates ex ante would be 15% less then AT&M and use the same three-level prices.
- AT&M's price cut would be for the entire Austria market, not just this region.

Costs

- Mobile telecommunications is a high-fixed cost, zero marginal-cost business.

- The cost structure of all providers is essentially the same (start-up costs, operating costs, licensing, etc).
- Incumbent providers generally have a customer acquisition costs that are 25% lower than new entrants do (acquisitions cost average €100 in other launch markets outside Austria).

Products

- Austria Star will launch with the latest 3G (broadband) technology that transmits data 2x faster than AT&Ms network.

Other information

- The managing partner on the account is on vacation and can't be reached for three days. However, you teammates can be reached immediately.
- The CEO of Austria Star is on route to Austria and will arrive at his office at 9:30 a.m.

Solution

The thing to recognize is that AT&M (the incumbent) is signaling that they will defend the market at most any cost (they are dropping rates in the entire country not just this market). This makes price-based competition is less appealing and product differentiation more important.

Another insight is the high market share of AT&M. This may actually prevent them from lowering prices as they have pledged because of antitrust law, which prevents predatory pricing to fend of new entrants in most countries.

Finally, as the industry is characterized by high fixed costs and zero variable costs, the client can reexamine their pricing strategy.

Armed with these insights, you tell the CEO that you will have a proposed response strategy ready for him and his communications team to review once he arrives in Austria. You tell him that despite the worrying nature of the news, there are three elements which can limit the negative effects:

- Firstly, as AT&M is announcing a price-based competition, you can focus on product differentiation instead. For example, you can emphasize that Austria Star offers twice the network speed, and promise superior service, which has been poor with the incumbent.

- Secondly, the zero variable cost nature of the industry provides you with flexibility to adjust your pricing strategy based on the news. You will reexamine the previous optimum in the coming hours and provide a new recommendation.

- Thirdly, the AT&M announcement can be deemed anti-competitive and even a breach of antitrust law. Incumbents which dominate market shares are generally not allowed to undercut prices when a new entrant launches in their market. This can be used both in a public response, and also as a response strategy by flagging this behavior with competitive authorities.

After concluding the call with the CEO, you also email the managing partner, outlining what has happened and the planned next steps.

Case #51: Chemical sweetener

Question

Your client manufactures a chemical sweetener used in beverages and other food products. The chemical will come off patent in one year. You have been asked to predict what might happen to the profitability of this product when the product comes off patent.

Information to be given if asked:

Product

- This is the only product of its kind, in terms of taste and safety (lack of harmful health effects) as proven in lab tests.
- The brand name of the product has slowly become a common household word.

Customers

- The largest two customers (75% of your sales) are two worldwide beverage companies.
- The companies feature the brand name of your client's chemical on their product, and consider it a sign of quality.

- The cost of the chemical sweetener represents 1.5% of their total costs.

Costs

- The costs to manufacture the product are extremely low (about 20% of the price of the product).
- Currently, the margins on this chemical are almost 40%.

Solution

This is a classic customer analysis problem. While most products that come off patent quickly drop in price (e.g. pharmaceuticals), this product will be able to retain some of its premium due to the strong brand name. Because the major two customers feature the chemical name on their product, and because the chemical represents such a small portion of their total costs, they can be expected to be willing to continue to pay the premium into the future. Therefore, the outlook for the product is good even after the patent expires.

Case #52: Chewing gum

Question

How would you estimate the size of the annual U.S. chewing gum market? Check your answer for reasonableness.

Solution

Estimate the number of people who chew gum: of the 300 million population, 15% are between the ages of 10 and 20, the heaviest users, for a total of 45 million. Estimate that these people chew two packs per week, for annual sales of 4,500 million packs. For the other users over age 20, (70% of the 300 million population, or 210 million) estimate a usage rate of one half pack per week, for a total of 5,250 million packs per year. Total packs per year is 9,750 million, or approximately 10 billion.

To check for reasonableness, figure the dollar sales that these packs represent: at 25 cents per pack, annual sales would be $2.5 billion, a reasonable figure.

Case #53: Gas plants

Question

This question was asked by McKinsey in a 2nd round interview.

Your client is a gas manufacturer. Currently the client owns and operates its gas plants nationwide. They have hired McKinsey to investigate whether they should enter into the business of running 3rd party gas plants. How will you structure the analysis of this case? Should the client enter or not enter into this business?

Information to be given if asked:

Customer Information

- The client manufactures hydrogen, oxygen etc.
- The customers are other industrial goods companies which use gas for producing steel, waste treatment etc.
- Some of the steel mills and waste treatment agencies own their own gas plants. For instance, a steel mill can have its own gas plant, which is located right next to the steel mill. These are the gas plants that the client

wants to operate (not buy them, just provide operations service)

- The client has highest market share in the market (about 30%).
- The market grows pretty much along with the GDP (1-3%).
- The cost of the gas for the customers is a small % of their total direct production costs. It is extremely important for the customers to have an uninterrupted supply of gas, since their steel plant shutdown is extremely expensive for them.

Firm's current economics

- The product is a commodity, so the firm is a price taker. The firm's revenues grow with GDP.
- Client's cost structure is the lowest in the industry.
- Think about how the gas plant's cost structure will change if the client operates it:
- Direct Material (DM) – raw material is air, which is free
- Direct Labor (DL) – very lean operation. One gas plant can be run by 1-2 persons. There will be no change.

- SG&A – Some reduction due to client's scale
- O/H – Some reduction by centralized monitoring and repair crew. Possible due to client's large scale of operations.

Client's resources/capabilities

- They have perfected the technique of monitoring the gas plants (using remote monitoring) and have the minimum average plant downtime/breakdown in the industry.
- By being the largest producer of gas, the client has achieved the highest economies of scale.

Competitive landscape and current issues

- There are 3 other national firms that manufacture and provide gas. Their market shares are smaller than that of our client.

Solution

The client can create value by operating 3rd party gas plants by lowering the operational cost somewhat. More importantly by minimizing the downtime of the gas plants they can add more significant value. Therefore, based on the value proposition, the client should enter into this business.

The client then needs to consider barriers to entry for other firms and implementation strategy.

Barriers to Entry

- The client's capabilities are unique in the industry. They can sign exclusive long term contracts with 3rd party clients to operate the gas plants.
- The client also needs to consider their pricing very carefully.

Implementation

- Evaluate the capital investment of this market entry.
- Since the client's infrastructure is well established, the capital cost will be minimal.

- The client could offer to operate 3rd party gas plants which are located reasonably close to their own plants. This would allow the client to go up the learning curve while ensuring uninterrupted gas supply to the customers.

Summary

The client should enter this market since there is value to be captured and the capital investment is low.

Case #54: Corn feed

Question

A corn feed company has eight manufacturing plants located in the Midwest. These plants service the entire United States. Their plant in Ohio needs refurbishing. The company has four possible options:

1. Refurbish the existing plant

2. Build a larger plant at the current location

3. Build a similar size plant at a new location

4. Build a larger plant at a new location

Which is the best option for this plant?

<u>Information to be given if asked:</u>

Market

- There are four main competitors; our plant is the second largest.
- All four competitors have similar manufacturing processes and similar cost structure.

Capacity

Capacity utilization at the current Ohio plant is 65%, which is industry standard.

Customers

- The current customers buy from all four manufacturers in order to guarantee supply.
- Currently demand is being met and there are no alternative uses for corn feed.

Transportation Costs

- The transportation cost for the corn stock (raw material) is much higher than the cost of transporting the actual feed.
- The corn is grown in the Ohio area and the feed is sold to the East Coast.

Product

The raw material is perishable whereas the corn feed can be stored for any length of time and easier to transport.

Solution

There are two issues to this decision. The plant size and the plant location should be considered separately.

1. Size of Plant

Corn feed is a commodity product. Pricing on the product is dependent on current corn prices as opposed to the manufacturing process. The purposed largest plant will not have economies of scales not currently present at the existing plant. Without increased economies of scale, there is no reason to increase the size of the plant.

2. Location of Plant

Transportation cost and perishability are the main issues with location. Cost analysis of the transportation cost of feed versus raw materials should be completed. This analysis should include the % of spoilage for longer transportation of corn stock.

In summary, the current plant is located close to the cornfields and this is the best location for the plant from the cost/benefit analysis. A larger plant should not be built.

Case #55: Scientific instruments

Question

A manufacturer of scientific instruments is experiencing declining sales in its major product line. Why?

<u>Information to be given if asked:</u>

Products

- The instrument, call it Y, is able to perform elemental mapping; that is, it is able to determine the specific composition of material placed in the chamber for observation. Y is an accessory for larger and much more expensive instrument that functions almost exactly like a microscope, which we'll call X.
- Our client's product is regarded as one of the best in the market.
- Aside from Y, the client recently began manufacturing X. Additionally, it produces an unrelated product.
- Product X can be used by itself, but Product Y is essentially dependent on Product X for its

operation. As a result, except for replacement sales, Y is rarely sold individually. In fact, Product X's sales force will frequently recommend that a buyer purchase a certain Y while buying an X. Two years ago, over 30% of our client's sales were generated by another manufacturer of X.

- The client's product X competes directly with other manufacturers of X, and particularly the manufacturer that was selling our Y. The client introduced X 1 1/2 years ago.

Sales

- Currently, 5% of sales come from recommendations from other manufactures.
- The markets for X and Y are flat.

Customers/Demographics

- There are two basic user groups: industry, primarily semiconductor manufacturers, and academia (in research labs).
- What we've noticed lately is that the specific users in each of these groups, who also happen to be the primary buyers, have become relatively less sophisticated; that is,

they are hired just to run the instruments and know less about their technical qualities.

- These buyers have become even more dependent on the sales forces.
- What has happened is that our client alienated itself from other manufacturers of X at a time when a strong relationship was becoming even more important than it used to be. The buyers are relying more and more on the X sales force, which are typically called well in advance of the Y sales force.

Solution

After using a strategic framework to unearth the
information above, the reason for declining sales
becomes clear:

In addition to ruining their relationships with
manufacturers of X by producing their own, the
client happened to do so at a time when
relationships became even more important.

Case #56: Fashion magazine

Question

Your client is a major fashion magazine that has been offered by its printer a proprietary new process called selective binding which enables publishers to customize the pages included in readers' magazines based on demographic data known about the reader. For example, an ad in Better Homes & Gardens for lawn chemical services could be placed only in those issues going to subscribers who live in houses and not to those living in condominiums or apartments. In this way, advertisers can focus their communications on the demographic segment they are targeting. Would you advise your client to take advantage of this new process and offer selective binding to its advertisers?

Information to be given if asked:

Readers

- The magazine's database can make demographic breakdowns between subscribers who make under $50,000 and those who make over $50,000.

- There are l million readers, 80% of who are subscribers.
- Twenty-five percent of subscribers make under $50×000, 75% make over $50,000. The same mix applies to the newsstand buyers according to readership audits.

Advertisers

- Most advertisers are selling high-end fashion products, so 75% of them are targeting the high-income group.

Costs

- The service is being offered to your client free for 3 years since the printer wants to promote the service's use by getting a major magazine to start using it.
- The client charges $50 per thousand per full-page ad (selective binding can only be offered on full-page ads). Therefore, revenue associated with a single inserted page (front and back) in an issue is $100 per thousand.

Competition

- The client's closest direct competitor has 500,000 readers, 100% of whom are subscribers. Effectively, all of their readers make over $50,000. They charge $70 per thousand for their full one-page ads.

Solution

The magazine would want to consider offering the service to its advertisers if it would be able to enhance its earnings by being able to charge its advertisers a premium for being able to more exactly and efficiently target the demographic segment they want to reach. Of course, the increased revenue from the any premium must be able to offset any revenue lost as advertisers stopped targeting.

Cost/Benefit Analysis

Since the printing cost to the client of selective binding is zero, the client needs to evaluate cost on the basis of revenue per thousand gained or lost as their advertiser base uses the service to better target their ads to their desired segment.

Presumably, instead of 100% of advertisers paying the full $50/thousand per page, the 25% of advertisers targeting the lower income segment will choose to advertise only to the 25% of subscribers targeting the high-income segment will choose to advertise only to the 25% of subscribers falling into that segment and the 75% of the advertisers targeting the high-income segment will advertise only to the high income subscribers (75% of subscribers). Assume that all advertisers continue to advertise in 100% of the newsstand copies. The revenue effect of this change can be calculated by looking at the impact the change would have on average ad rate per thousand on subscription readership:

New ad revenue per page = Old ad revenue per page X [(% low income subscribers X % low income target advertisers) + (% high income subscribers X % high income advertisers)]

Thus, new ad revenue per page = $50 X [(25% X 25%) + (75% X 75%)] at old rate $31.25 < $50

Now the question is, can ad rates per thousand on the selective binding portion of ads sold be increased sufficiently to increase average revenue per thousand over what it is today? To answer this question, your client's ad rates must be looked at from the perspective of their advertisers. If you consider the advertisers targeting the high-income group, their alternative to advertising in your client's magazine is to put their ad dollars toward the 100% high-income readership competitor. The cost per thousand high-income readers with the competitor magazine is:

(Page rate X total readership)/ (portion of readers who are high income) = ($70 X 500,000)/500,000 = $70

Thus $70 is the maximum price per thousand the client can charge its advertisers for selectively bound ads before the advertisers would switch to their competitor. Note that currently, the client is a cheaper buy for these high-income advertisers even though they are paying to reach readers they do not want:

($50 X 1 million)/750,000 = $66.67

If the client charged $70/thousand for selectively bound ads, average revenue per thousand to the client would be:

$70 X [(25% X 25%) + (75% X 75%)) = $43.75

Conclusion

Since $43.75 is less than the $50 that advertisers are currently paying, the magazine should not offer advertisers the selective binding service.

Of course, there are other issues which interviewees might want to mention such as the possibility of price discriminating between high and low-income advertisers, the potential for and cost of expanding the advertising base using selective binding as a selling tool, etc. However, it is important by the end of the interview to have reached a recommendation regarding the initial question posed by the interviewer. To mention these other possibilities and areas for further investigation is certainly worthwhile, but it is also important not to get too far off track or to complicate the issue so much that a final recommendation is never reached.

Case #57: Candy

Question

Your company is a rather successful producer of candy. It originally started as a single product line. The production process consists of two basic activities: manufacturing and packaging. The firm has also expanded its sales through product line extensions. Management is concerned that sales are growing but profits are not increasing at the same rate. What can your company do?

Information to be given if asked:

Raw materials are commodities with cyclical prices which have fallen in recent years, but are expected to swing up again.

Labor and fixed capital costs per unit have increased compared to ten years ago.

The company's controlling system still focuses on the manufacturing part of production and the cost explosion occurs in packaging (the product line extension is primarily adding new types of packaging)

Controlling processes are focused on manufacturing, which is rather efficient already, but not packaging, thus causing slack in labor and fixed capital (small batch sizes, high setup times)

There are a number of other issues: concentration of retailers, trade brands, retailers demand large introductory discounts for new products, high failure rate of new products.

Solution

After learning about all the issues, i.e. by using the Profitability framework, you can suggest a number of potential actions:

- Reduce product variety if customers (retailers) are willing to accept the reduced selection
- Reduce low margin trade brand production
- Explore opportunities for increased automation to reduce labor costs
- Analyze utilization of tooling, equipment and factory floor space, to find opportunities to reduce fixed costs
- Emphasize pull marketing, reduce introduction rate for new products
- Introduce controlling/scheduling measures for packaging

Case #58: Cola

Question

RC Cola and Coca Cola both compete in the same industry. Their cost structures are vastly different, however. Using Coca Cola as a benchmark, estimate the likely cost structure for RC Cola. In other words, for which costs would RC Cola be higher, for which would they be lower, and why?

Solution

This is a twist on the standard price/cost case that also questions the interviewee's understanding of the cost items. A possible analysis, line item by line item:

Cost

- RC Cola would be higher due to their lesser power in negotiating price breaks from suppliers.

Distribution

- RC is not distributed in as many outlets as Coca Cola. Therefore, the average truck driver will be driving more miles and spending more time to deliver a truckload of RC that the Coca Cola driver, who will have several stops within an immediate area.
- Also, the typical order size for RC Cola would be smaller, meaning that more stops would have to be made. In the case of Coca Cola, it is conceivable that one truckload may be delivered to just one customer.

Sales

- Could be lower for RC, as there are fewer, but
  more loyal customers.

Marketing

- Lower for RC Cola, as they are not a frequent
  advertiser like Coca Cola.

Administration / Overhead

- Lower for RC Cola, as they are more of a "one-
  product" company than is Coca Cola.

Case #59: Banking branch

Question

How would you determine whether a location in New York City holds enough banking demand to warrant opening a branch?

Hint

Because this is a demand-oriented question, you should consider a marketing framework, such as the 4 P's.

Solution

The demographics of the area surrounding the prospective branch should be examined. Population, business concentration, income levels, etc. should be compared with those of historically successful branches.

Competitor reactions could easily make this venture unprofitable, so it is essential to anticipate them. These will depend on the importance of the area to competitors (in terms of profit, share, etc.)

The client will have to match competitors' incentives to customers and should estimate the cost of doing so.

The client must examine if the new branch would complement their existing competence and strategy (retail or commercial, high growth or high profitability, etc.) and what purpose it would serve. If the need focuses on deposits and withdrawals only, maybe a cash machine would suffice.

Case #60: Calling centers

Question

You have a have recently been assigned to a project with one of the nation's super regional banks. The bank is one of the top 10 largest retail banks in the country. Like most banks in its class it has branches in 8 geographically contiguous states.

Your client has recently concluded that the old "local branch" way of business is no longer viable. Typically, this bank has canvassed its territory with small freestanding branches; however, the new age of electronic banking and commerce is changing all of that.

They are considering replacing many branches with Calling Centers. Calling Centers offer both live and phone automated services that may be accessed by phone. The new Centers would offer virtually all of the services currently offered through local branches plus some additional things.

The question to you is: how would you go about setting up the engagement to determine the viability of this new concept? Specifically, what

kinds of things would you investigate? And what
hypothesis would you form?

Solution

It is recommended to structure the solution as a cost benefit analysis. The number of new customers times the expected revenue from them plus the additional revenue generated by potential new services plus the cost savings must outweigh the forgone revenue generated by the customers you end up driving away.

This is a very open broad-brushed case. There certainly is no right answer; however, this type of case occurs frequently. The following is a guideline of some things you should probably consider:

Market analysis

- What kinds of customers would be attracted to this no service?
- What kinds of customers would be turned off? (Hypothesis: younger people would be heavier users and more attracted than older)
- Of the people attracted to this new service, how profitable are they?
- How profitable are the people who are turned off by this service? (Hypothesis: older people

have more money and thus are more profitable)

Revenue

- What types of new services could be added to increase revenues?
- Automatic bill payment, Fund transfer, etc.

Cost Savings

- How much would it cost to establish a Calling Center and what are the risks involved?
- Do we have the expertise in-house to do this?
- How many branches could we close?
- Can we cut down on traffic to existing branches - thus requiring fewer tellers?